frail HAPPINESS

frail HAPPINESS

AN ESSAY ON
ROUSSEAU

TZVETAN TODOROV

TRANSLATED BY
JOHN T. SCOTT *and* ROBERT D. ZARETSKY

The Pennsylvania State University Press
University Park, Pennsylvania

Cet ouvrage publié dans le cadre du programme d'aide à la publication bénéficie du soutien du Ministère des Affaires Etrangères et du Service Culturel de l'Ambassade de France représenté aux Etats-Unis.

This work, published as part of the program of aid for publication, received support from the French Ministry of Foreign Affairs and the Cultural Service of the French Embassy in the United States.

Library of Congress Cataloging-in-Publication Data

Todorov, Tzvetan, 1939–
    [Frêle bonheur. English]
    Frail happiness : an essay on Rousseau / Tzvetan Todorov ; translated by John T. Scott and Robert D. Zaretsky.
        p. cm.
    Includes bibliographical references.
    ISBN 0-271-02110-1 (cloth : alk. paper)
    1. Rousseau, Jean-Jacques, 1712–1778. I. Title.

B2137 .T5713 2001
    194—dc21

                                        00-067600

First published in France as *Frêle bonheur: Essai sur Rousseau*
© Hachette, 1985

English translation © 2001 The Pennsylvania State University
All rights reserved.
Printed in the United States of America
Published by The Pennsylvania State University Press,
University Park, PA 16802-1003

CONTENTS

As with all great writers, Jean-Jacques Rousseau has not one, but multiple, facets. One can love him—or hate him—for very different reasons. Some readers see him foremost as the master of French prose, and it is certainly difficult to resist his style, no less multifaceted than the author himself. Consider the great distance between the dazzling formulas in his *Discourse on the Origin of Inequality* and the extremely spare, scarcely audible words in *Reveries of the Solitary Walker*! Other readers are attracted to the fearless explorer of the self—the author of the first true autobiographical quest, which would be endlessly copied and imitated during the two centuries from his death up to our time. As for me, the Rousseau I cherish more than any other is the thinker who provides an amazingly acute and lucid analysis of the human condition.

In the history of European thought, Rousseau comes to light as one of the principal spokesmen for humanism. What I find most valuable in his thought is not just his articulation of humanist principles—though he is the first to express them with such vigor—but also his capacity both to imagine and to explore their consequences, conjunctions, and possible perversions. (Contrary to what is often said, Rousseau was no dreamer.) Take, for example, the primordial imperative of all humanists: the autonomy of the subject. By insisting too much on the individual's autonomy, do we not risk ending up as a collection of monads, of self-sufficient entities, of beings who do not really live in society? It has often been thought, even with reference to Rousseau himself, that this is the curse of the Moderns. After all, didn't he imagine a "state of nature" in which human beings led solitary lives? But this is to read too hastily, for Rousseau notes that in such a "state of nature," man is not yet fully human. He becomes such only after having won the attention of other men. It is through becoming aware of the existence of others that he discovers his own existence. It is through becoming aware of the diversity of men that he reaches the continent of good and evil and realizes that he is free to perform one or the other. Indeed, it is only at this point that man leaves behind the animal condition and can be properly called "human." Far from forming themselves into self-sufficient entities, human beings are born, live, and die in a state of incompleteness, with a deep need for others. It is their gaze, Rousseau affirms, that allows us to exist.

Or let us take ennobling an individual, as we do in love and friendship, as the utmost aim of our actions. The novelty of humanist thought since Montaigne is to conceive of these relationships in an intransitive manner. When I love an individual, it is not because he is the incarnation of beauty or virtue, as the ancient Greeks would have it, or because it is through him that I express my love for God, as Christian thinkers from Saint Augustine to Pascal recommended. Instead, I love him because he is himself. Purely human love is the transcendence of our disenchanted world. "But," immediately retort those of a sarcastic bent, "isn't this a paltry sort of transcendence? Doesn't it essentially admit that we must be content with illusions, with self-willed illusions, since each and every one of us knows that the qualities of the beloved are, in essence, the work of the lover's imagination? By giving our actions exclusively human aims, do we not condemn ourselves to a kind of mediocrity?"

Rousseau is well aware of what occupies the indulgent imagination of the lover (the process of "crystallization" dear to Stendhal was well known to the moralists of the seventeenth century and, before them, to the ancient Latin writers). But it is not enough for him to denounce our vain illusions. While it is true that absolute Beauty and God have disappeared, the distinguishing feature of human beings—and, at the same time, their merit—is the ability to convert the relative into an absolute, to transform the dross of common mediocrity into the gold of authentic feelings. In the infinite love of the father for his child, or the love of the lover for his beloved, it is not the object of the love that is admirable, but the love itself. "The love that I know," Rousseau writes, "is inflamed by the image of the illusory perfection of the beloved object; this very illusion leads it to enthusiasm for virtue." Perfection is illusory, but not the love to which it gives birth: therein lies the essential.

The pages Rousseau devotes to morality can sometimes seem old-fashioned. Nowadays we do not like to be preached to, even by people with good intentions. However, Rousseau's moral teaching is not lax, nor is it intimidating. Altruism is preferable to selfishness, but preference for another does not require doing violence to oneself. The good can be approached in two ways: by way of goodness or by way of virtue. It is true that the latter route implies that we must overcome certain desires or predilections in order to conform to duty. But the former route, which Rousseau himself prefers, leads to the same goal by encouraging us to abandon ourselves to our desire to please others. Being the "relative" beings we are, we find our happiness in the happiness of those we love. "We do everything we can for our friends as we do for ourselves, not because of duty but because of the delight it brings us." Happiness and the good, far from being incompatible, can be combined.

The popular image of Rousseau is that of a man who takes his dreams for reality and takes pleasure in an idyllic vision of humanity. Nothing could be further from the truth in his writings. Human beings are neither good nor evil; they are free and hence capable (especially) of the worst. Social through and through, they can only deceive themselves by pretending to suffice unto themselves or to love only God. But with indispensable attachments come possible frustration and inevitable suffering. "It is much more from our affections than from our needs that the troubles of our lives are born." The beings we love—through whom we live— can change, stop loving us or stop being lovable, or die. We have no recourse against this "imperfection" (this finitude) of human beings. Multiplying our attachments or constantly changing their object would condemn us to an even more desperate plunge forward. Rousseau accepts our purely human world, but this world does not inspire joy in him. Just as in love, what we can admire in the end is not the human condition such as he depicts it, but the rigor with which he grasps even its most tragic tensions.

Tzvetan Todorov

I.

For the first quarter-century of his life, Tzvetan Todorov lived under the kind of regime for which Jean-Jacques Rousseau has often been faulted, denounced as its intellectual forefather. Born in Sofia in 1939, Todorov was still a child when the Bulgarian Communist Party took power following the execution of members of the former government. The country remained in the deep freeze of Stalinist rule in 1963, when Todorov arrived in Paris to further his study in literary theory. A temporary stay became permanent, and Todorov eventually acquired both French citizenship and an international reputation as a structuralist. In a series of works published in the 1960s and 1970s, Todorov not only introduced important Eastern European and Russian literary theorists to the West—such as Roman Jakobson and Mikhail Bakhtin—but

The translators wish to thank Peter Potter and Laura Reed-Morrisson at The Pennsylvania State University Press for the enthusiasm, intelligence, and care that they have shown through the entire editorial process.

also helped lay the theoretical foundation for the discipline of poetics.[1]

By the early 1980s, Todorov began to turn his attention to history and to political thought. The areas of his attention have been varied: the "discovery" and conquest of the Americas by the Europeans; the behavior of men and women in Nazi and Soviet concentration camps; the tragedy of French and Jewish hostages in a small town in France during the first days of Liberation; the reevaluation of the thought of Benjamin Constant. At first glance, these concerns may seem thoroughly unrelated to the study of language. Yet to these moral, historical, and political essays, Todorov has carried over his search for an objective and universal footing—a footing he previously sought in a "science" of literature. He insists upon a universal standard by which political theorists or historians can judge the acts of fellow men and women.[2] This continuity of concern and analysis is clearest in his work on French philosophers and thinkers. In a manner that recalls the best work of intellectual historians of earlier generations, he has engaged in dialogue the great figures of French moral and political theory. From his 1989 analysis of nationalism, racism, and exoticism in *On Human Diversity* to his 1999 study of humanist thought in France, *The Imperfect Garden*, Todorov has traced the modern humanist tradition with a particular emphasis on French intellectuals. In doing so, he has also sought to construct a "critical

1. See Tzvetan Todorov, *Introduction to Poetics*, trans. Richard Howard (Minneapolis: University of Minnesota Press, 1982), and his introduction to *French Literary Theory Today*, trans. R. Carter (Cambridge: Cambridge University Press, 1982).

2. For a fuller exploration of this evolution in Todorov's writing, see Robert Zaretsky, "*Tragédies bulgares et françaises:* Tzvetan Todorov and the Writing of History," in *France at War: Vichy France and the Historians*, ed. Sarah Fishman et al. (London: Berg, 2000), and "Tzvetan Todorov and the Writing of History," *South Central Review* 15, no. 3–4 (1998–99), 30–37. This issue of *South Central Review* is devoted to the work of Todorov. For a useful overview of Todorov's career, see Jean Verrier, *Tzvetan Todorov: Du formalisme russe aux morales de l'histoire* (Paris: Bertrande-Lacoste, 1995).

humanism." In this effort at reconsidering the humanist legacy, Todorov has examined the work of thinkers from Montaigne to Lévi-Strauss, paying special attention to Montaigne, Montesquieu, and Constant.[3]

The figure of Jean-Jacques Rousseau nonetheless eclipses even this philosophical trio in Todorov's analysis of humanism. The paradox of Rousseau's centrality is apparent; as Todorov himself notes at the start of *Frail Happiness,* he had long felt a "certain reticence" concerning the "intellectual extremism" he and many other readers have found in Rousseau's thought. Perhaps for this very reason, Todorov has been repeatedly drawn to this tormented, restless, and puzzling thinker. It is not surprising that *Frail Happiness* is one of the earliest works in the second phase of Todorov's intellectual career. Our purpose, in this introduction, is to show how Rousseau and Todorov cast light on one another's thought. A summary of Todorov's inquiry into the humanist tradition will be followed by a discussion of his interpretation of Rousseau.

II.

Ever since the early 1980s and the publication of *The Conquest of America,* Todorov has sought to conceptualize how we understand—and *ought* to understand—our fellow human beings and ourselves. Though the dual tasks of analyst and moralist are difficult to reconcile, he has claimed the two roles with enthusiasm. For example, in *On Human Diversity,* he explains that his analysis is "a hybrid, half history of thought, half essay in moral and political philosophy." He is concerned with the meaning of his authors'

3. While Montesquieu and Tocqueville figure in Todorov's broad historical surveys, he has devoted an entire book to the thought of Constant: *Benjamin Constant: La Passion démocratique* (Paris: Hachette, 1997), translated as *A Passion for Democracy* (New York: Agora Publishing, 1999).

texts and with their "truth value."[4] Todorov's emphasis upon the moral obligations of the historian and political thinker is a central element in his effort to build a critical humanism (as he calls it in that work).

He was, in fact, engaged in this project long before he ever gave it a name. As early as *The Conquest of America* and *Frail Happiness*, Todorov sought a coherent view of an intellectual tradition that has allowed both the horrors of modern history and a critique of those very events. There are certain traits running through most, if not all, of Todorov's works that characterize his sense of critical humanism. First, there is the attention that Todorov pays to the particular and the specific—a quality he discovers in Rousseau. According to Todorov, Rousseau practices a universalism that does not "deduce human identity from a principle, whatever it may be; rather, it starts by becoming thoroughly familiar with the particular, and then progresses by feeling its way. . . . The universal is the horizon of understanding between *two* particulars."[5] This "horizon" necessarily stretches across history, reaching, for example, Dutch painting of the Golden Age of the seventeenth century. Todorov argues that the Dutch masters' eye for detail and the everyday are not simply aesthetic choices but also moral choices. Artists like Steen, Ter Borch, de Hooch, Vermeer, and Hals, "rather than comforting us with welcome illusions, teach us to see the world more clearly. They do not invent beauty, but discover it—and invite us, in our turn, to discover it. Threatened today by new forms of degradation in our everyday lives, we are tempted upon looking at these paintings to rediscover the sense and beauty of the most fundamental gestures."[6]

4. *On Human Diversity: Nationalism, Racism, and Exoticism in French Thought*, trans. Catherine Porter (Cambridge: Harvard University Press, 1993), xiii–xiv. Translation of *Nous et les autres: La Réflexion française sur la diversité humaine* (Paris: Le Seuil, 1989).

5. Ibid., 12.

6. *Eloge du quotidien* (Paris: Le Seuil, 1997), 145.

Yet while Todorov values details for their own sake, details also lead us to common and, at times, universal qualities. The invariable shift from the particular to the general is a second important trait in his work. Just as his earlier work in poetics is grounded in the belief that a particular text exemplifies the general laws of narrative art, so too is the more recent work inspired by the belief that general conditions of *moral* meaning must exist if we are to understand historical events. This axiomatic belief not only serves as a tool of analysis but also provides an ethical perspective that has remained a constant in his writings. This helps explain his impatience, for example, with the American culture wars fought by what he labels "relativists" and "particularists." With refreshing good sense, he reminds both camps that the essence of being human "is not just to have particular interests, but also to be capable of going beyond these same interests."[7]

More important, the constant play that Todorov maintains between the particular and the general illuminates the motivations of men and women in times of moral crisis. In both *Facing the Extreme* and *A French Tragedy*, he makes admirable use of the *ethics of conviction* and the *ethics of responsibility* (categories first proposed by Max Weber) in order to explain and privilege certain ethical acts over others. There exists, Todorov argues, a critical distinction between heroic and ordinary virtues. While the former value abstract principles and grand gestures, the latter never lose sight of individual human beings. Dignity and caring are two essential expressions of the ordinary virtues; dignity entails human agency— the ability to match one's actions with one's will—while caring is the ability to recognize the other, regardless of his or her relationship to oneself, as a fellow human being worthy of respect and help. The ordinary virtues begin and end with other, particular human beings precisely because they acknowledge certain univer-

7. *L'Homme dépaysé* (Paris: Le Seuil, 1996), 209.

sal values. (As we will see, these notions also inform his concept of a critical humanism—and Rousseau's role in that humanism.)

Finally, the movement between the particular and universal also plays an important role in Todorov's controversial distinction between literal history and exemplary history. *Literal history* refers uniquely to itself, becoming an event that ultimately serves to define an individual or group. It remains "an intransitive fact."[8] On the other hand, *exemplary history* allows for the singularity of an event—but not its uniqueness. Not an incommensurable event (one that is often sacralized), it instead serves as a model. It is a memory that opens itself "to analogy and generalization . . . an *exemplum* from which one draws lessons."[9] While literal history leads to ritual and commemoration, exemplary history encourages communication.

The emphasis upon dialogue is another core element of Todorov's work. At times, it emerges in the form of conversations with contemporaries, as with the literary theorists Paul Bénichou and Ian Watt.[10] Todorov claims that the only valid criticism is dialogical, the "meeting of two voices: the author's and critic's, neither one is privileged over the other."[11] But this is an ideal, a regulative principle that, in practice, can never be realized. All such dialogues are asymmetrical, since the text is "closed" and, often, the author is dead. As a result, Todorov affirms the need to make the author's voice heard as clearly and faithfully as possible. This explains the generous length and frequency of his quotations: they help reestablish a balance undone by the passage of time. Yet, in the end,

8. *Les Abus de la mémoire* (Paris: Arléa, 1995), 30.

9. Ibid., 30. In the original French version of *Facing the Extreme*, trans. Arthur Denner and Abigail Pollack (New York: Holt, 1996), Todorov uses the term "paradigmatic," which may give a more accurate sense of the notion than the word "exemplum" does in the translated version.

10. See *Critique de la critique* (Paris: Le Seuil, 1984), translated by Catherine Porter as *Literature and Its Theorists* (Ithaca: Cornell University Press, 1987).

11. Ibid., 185.

there is no end to the conversation. According to Todorov, authentic dialogue neither comes into full possession of the truth nor renounces the quest; instead, it serves as a meeting ground between artist and critic, past and present, conservative and liberal, human being and human being. In *On Human Diversity*, he expands upon this notion: "The word that best characterizes my project (if not its execution), I find, is 'dialogue.' This implies, above all, that I am not interested solely in the meaning of my authors' texts . . . but that I am also interested in their truth value. It is not enough for me to have identified their arguments . . . I also attempt to find out whether I can accept those arguments."[12] In short, for Todorov there is a critical difference between a conversation and a dialogue; the latter implies the presence of a common ground or horizon that allows for the very possibility of argument.

An increasingly compelling element in Todorov's work is his use of autobiography. For example, he begins *On Human Diversity* with a terse recollection: early in his life he had "met evil." Having grown up under the oppressive weight of the communist regime in Bulgaria and the corruption of language that it fostered, he encountered its odd duplication in France, where he soon discovered that an equally dispiriting gap existed (especially on the Left) between language and reality. As a result, he decided to try to understand both "how things have been but also how they ought to be. Not one *or* the other, but both one *and* the other."[13] He reemphasizes his personal stake and moral focus in the interpretive essay that introduces the accounts of the men and women imprisoned and tortured by the Bulgarian regime in the late 1950s and early 1960s. He affirms that this "horror was part of my world, but I did not know that [these camps] existed. . . . I am not now seeking to escape my guilt, since I know that I have nothing in particular

---

12. *On Human Diversity*, xiv–xv.
13. Ibid., vii, xi.

for which I ought to feel guilty. Nevertheless . . . I will never be able to say that these stories do not concern me."[14]

This list of qualities is far from exhaustive, but it suffices to reveal some of the reasons for Todorov's attraction to Rousseau as well as the role played by the latter in Todorov's notion of a critical humanism. Both men know the nature of being the "other" (both lived in France as foreigners, though, unlike Todorov, Rousseau's native tongue was French); both express impatience toward the disjunction between saying and doing; both pay great attention to the particulars of our lives—tempered by an abiding belief in certain universal values. Todorov approvingly quotes Rousseau's *Discourse on the Origin of Inequality:* "When it comes to thinking about human nature, the true Philosopher is neither an Indian nor a Tartar, neither from Geneva nor from Paris, but is a man."[15]

III.

Frail Happiness was the first work to appear after Todorov turned to the thinkers of the past. In the preface, Todorov explains that he had grown dissatisfied with the scholarly language of specialists and the divorce of professional discourse from the essential concerns of our everyday lives. He found in Rousseau and other thinkers a refreshingly direct elaboration of the concerns of modern life. Rousseau particularly attracted his attention, he explains, because "he both discovered and invented our modernity" (2). Rousseau discovered the modern condition that was emerging around him, and the vocabulary he developed to articulate that condition contains words and concepts that we still use today. An examination of Rousseau's thought would, then, be a way of re-

14. *Voices from the Gulag: Life and Death in Communist Bulgaria,* trans. Robert Zaretsky (University Park: The Pennsylvania State University Press, 1999).
15. *On Human Diversity,* 44.

flecting upon an important intellectual figure of modernity and upon the modern condition itself. Todorov therefore calls his investigation of Rousseau "practical," rather than philosophical or literary. Rousseau's thought provides a whetstone on which Todorov hones his philosophical tools, examining the questions that confront us.

Todorov explains that he was initially reticent about Rousseau's thought because he saw in it "a certain philosophical extremism" (3). Other readers from Rousseau's time to our own have been struck by that same extremism. Rousseau's name has been yoked to the French Revolution ever since the event—both by critics such as Edmund Burke and participants like Robespierre, as well as later analysts of the upheaval, especially the influential historian Hippolyte Taine. This reputation for insidious extremism has pursued Rousseau. In the aftermath of World War II, notable intellectuals as varied as Karl Popper and Bertrand Russell joined in a chorus excoriating Rousseau as the intellectual forerunner of the totalitarian experiments of the twentieth century. Rousseau is therefore widely held to be at fault for the evils that Todorov himself has confronted.[16]

Given his own personal experience, Todorov's interpretation of Rousseau as a central figure in modern humanism is a paradox worthy of Rousseau himself. Todorov altered his initial impression of Rousseau when he realized that his apparent extremism "was in fact sheer intensity of thought" (3). What he had taken to be extremism was actually Rousseau's pursuit of different lines of reasoning to their logical extremes. Rousseau's conclusions might be extreme, Todorov acknowledges, "but this does not mean that he simply accepts everything he says" (3). The apparent simplicity of language that first attracted Todorov to Rousseau turned out to

16. For Todorov's discussion of how the "evil" he experienced growing up in communist Bulgaria led him to turn to Rousseau and other thinkers, see the preface to *On Human Diversity*.

be misleading, for Rousseau articulates a complex reality and offers us different ways to negotiate it. The complexity of Rousseau's thought mirrors the complexity of modern life. In his dialogue with the thinker, Todorov concludes that he is indeed "at fault"— not for generating the extremes of modernity, but for being modernity's most insightful interlocutor.

The insight that Rousseau investigates several different "ways"[17] open to us in our modern condition is the key to Todorov's argument in *Frail Happiness*. By seeking to understand how the divergent philosophical paths Rousseau pursues could be the outcome of a single coherent theory, Todorov addresses the enduring question of the unity of Rousseau's thought. Rousseau himself proclaims the fundamental unity of his "system."[18] His readers are nonetheless confronted by works that seem discordant, if not simply contradictory. How can the solitary wanderer of the autobiographical writings be the author of the *Social Contract*? The debate over the unity of Rousseau's thought has preoccupied scholars for the last century, with such influential interpreters as Ernst Cassirer and Charles Hendel sustaining the cause of unity against a constant supply of readers who see disunity.[19] Framing his own reading of Rousseau in terms of a problem that the philosopher

17. Here, we have translated *"voie"* as "way," though *"voie"* might also be rendered as "path," as it is in Catherine Porter's translation of *On Human Diversity* (e.g., 178). We have chosen to use the term "way" in order to maintain Todorov's deliberate provocation: discussing a "third way" introduced by Rousseau into modern humanism evokes various attempts, usually antimodern and antihumanistic, to find an alternative to modern liberalism and socialism.

18. See Rousseau, *Lettre à Beaumont*, *O.C.*, Vol. 4, 928; *Dialogues*, First Dialogue, 22–23.

19. See Ernst Cassirer, *The Question of Jean-Jacques Rousseau*, trans. Peter Gay (New Haven: Yale University Press, 1963), originally published as "Das Problem Jean-Jacques Rousseau," *Archiv für Geschichte der Philosophie* 41 (1953), 177–213, 479–513. See also Charles Hendel, *Jean-Jacques Rousseau: Moralist*, 2 vols. (Oxford: Oxford University Press, 1934). For other contributions to the debate over the unity of Rousseau's thought, see the studies by Burgelin, Derathé, and Goldschmidt to which Todorov refers in the list of the scholarly works he consulted for *Frail Happiness* (p. 69 below).

diagnoses and a set of remedies that he entertains, Todorov joins a school of interpretation stemming from Rousseau's own statement of the core idea of his thought: nature made man good, and society corrupts him. While this is a recognizable approach to Rousseau, it permits a wide variety of interpretations. For instance, Jean Starobinski draws upon a psychoanalytic reading of Rousseau in order to argue that his thought is suffused with the problem of overcoming the obstacles that prevent us from regaining a lost "transparency" of existence.[20] Starobinski's influence on Todorov is perhaps most evident in the latter's discussion of Rousseau's autobiographical works. Todorov's approach is, however, more indebted to a group of interpreters who restrict themselves to Rousseau's philosophical works. Like Victor Goldschmidt, Roger D. Masters, and Alexis Philonenko,[21] among others, Todorov starts from the principles of Rousseau's theory as the philosopher himself explained them, and then seeks to understand how his thought as a whole grows out of them.

Todorov sets himself the task of exploring the architecture of Rousseau's thought. He therefore begins his essay by looking at the basic structure of the doctrine. Rousseau held that once we humans emerge from the primitive "state of nature" and irrevocably enter the "state of society," we find ourselves in a corrupt condition, torn between conflicting inclinations and duties. Dissatisfied with our current social state, we yearn for a state of nature forever gone. Since we cannot go back, we imagine a new condition where our ills will be remedied. This new condition is a third

20. See Jean Starobinski, *Jean-Jacques Rousseau: Transparency and Obstruction*, trans. Arthur Goldhammer (Chicago: University of Chicago Press, 1988), originally published as *Jean-Jacques Rousseau: La Transparence et l'obstacle* (Paris: Plon, 1957).

21. See Victor Goldschmidt, *Anthropologie et politique: Les Principes du système de Rousseau* (Paris: Vrin, 1974); Roger D. Masters, *The Political Philosophy of Rousseau* (Princeton: Princeton University Press, 1968); Alexis Philonenko, *Jean-Jacques Rousseau et la pensée du malheur,* 3 vols. (Paris: Vrin, 1984). See also Arthur M. Melzer, *The Natural Goodness of Man: On the System of Rousseau's Thought* (Chicago: University of Chicago Press, 1990).

"way," neither in the past nor in the present—an ideal that lies in the future. The third state contains the remedy "that will allow us to combat the previously diagnosed illness" (9). There is not a single remedy, however; indeed, the very multiplicity of ideals poses a problem for mankind as well as a hurdle to those who seek to comprehend Rousseau's thought. For Todorov, the central difficulty in understanding Rousseau is itself the secret to grasping the course and conclusions of his thought.

In pursuing the remedies contemplated by Rousseau, Todorov begins by following Rousseau's own suggestion that there are two opposing versions of the ideal individual: "man" and "citizen." A number of other prominent interpreters have also followed Rousseau down this path, including Judith Shklar.[22] Like Todorov, they have seen those different ideals as mutually exclusive, two autonomous models directed at conflicting goals. The choice between these two ideals is a choice between the divergent goals that we feel within ourselves in our corrupt social state. It seems that we must choose just one way, either that of "man" or that of "citizen." Rousseau nonetheless seems to follow both of these paths. In his own life he is alternately the "Citizen of Geneva" and the "solitary walker." And in his writings we see him address both of these antithetical identities. Rousseau's simultaneous adoption of these two opposing ways might be seen as evidence of a fundamental contradiction in his thought. Or it might be the result of the contradiction that Rousseau discerns in the human condition. Todorov embraces this second possibility. "If there is a contradiction, it is in the human condition; there is nothing contradictory in the act of observing and describing a contradiction" (19). Todorov insists that Rousseau is aware of the limitations, even the dangers, represented by the divergent ways of "man" and "citizen" that somehow converge within him.

22. See Judith Shklar, *Men and Citizens: A Study of Rousseau's Social Thought* (Cambridge: Cambridge University Press, 1969). See also Melzer, *The Natural Goodness of Man.*

A distinguishing mark of Todorov's reading of Rousseau is his argument about how Rousseau distances himself from the possibilities he describes. Todorov draws upon his training in literary theory by attending to the form of Rousseau's discourse. According to Todorov, "In order to speak about each of these ways, Rousseau adopts its particular perspective. To remove the impression of any contradiction, it is enough to note that he practices a kind of 'free indirect style'" (19). Rousseau may speak of these ways in his own voice, writing "I," but he is actually speaking in the name of the way or ideal that he is investigating at the time. In taking this interpretative tack, Todorov builds upon Leo Strauss's reading of Rousseau without adopting his views on Rousseau's esotericism.[23] Like Strauss, Todorov sees that Rousseau adopts multiple roles as author and contends that his arguments must be comprehended in terms of the role he is assuming at the time. Todorov extends this approach, however, to understand Rousseau's investigation of the different ways open to all human beings. Todorov argues that Rousseau lends his genius to each way in order to reveal its logic, taking each to its logical conclusion.

Todorov's approach to Rousseau's discourse can be seen in his discussion of the first two ways open to humankind. In his analysis of the *Social Contract* and Rousseau's other political writings, Todorov rejects the notion that Rousseau constructs a utopia or indulges in nostalgia for the ancient city of Athens or Rome that he knows is impossible to reconstruct in modern times.[24] The civic education and state surveillance that Rousseau says is necessary to form true citizens is all too possible—and characterizes contemporary totalitarian states. Todorov concludes that Rousseau offers the vision of the citizen to the Poles and others as a warning. "Champion of individual freedom and of the free determina-

23. See, in particular, Leo Strauss, "On the Intention of Rousseau," *Social Research* 14 (1947), 455–87. See also Strauss, *Natural Right and History* (Chicago: University of Chicago Press, 1955).

24. See, for example, Shklar, *Men and Citizens*.

tion of the subject, Rousseau does not advocate civic education for his contemporaries. Instead, he presents an 'if . . . then' analysis: if one assumes the perspective of the citizen, then this is what follows. Let those who are committed to this way be aware of the consequences of their actions" (25). The patriotism demanded of the citizen is, in fact, antithetical to the cosmopolitanism to which Rousseau's principles lead. Rousseau describes the "logic" of the citizen in order to show us that it must be rejected.

Having concluded that Rousseau looks through the citizen's lenses without approving what he sees, Todorov applies the same method of reading to Rousseau's description of the way of the solitary individual. The solitary individual is represented most notably by Rousseau himself. Todorov's contention that Rousseau can speak in his own name without necessarily adopting the perspective of that "I" is therefore a particularly difficult position to defend.[25] Rousseau flees persecution and seeks happiness in solitude, but Todorov asks whether Rousseau ever really sought absolute solitude. He finds that the way of the solitary individual described by Rousseau actually entails "limited communication," meaning by "communication" both literal communication and contact with humans and other beings more generally. In his solitude, Rousseau communicates through writing, through his imagination, and through the contemplation of nature, or he depersonalizes other beings so that communication with them does not threaten his own autonomy. Todorov sees a danger in these forms of communication essayed by Rousseau. He focuses in particular on depersonalization as a failure to recognize others as autonomous and equal subjects in their own right. Rousseau embraces the ideal of solitude as a remedy for the ills of society. "But,

25. For an exchange between Todorov and a critic who does not believe that he succeeds in making this interpretation, see *New Literary History* 27 (1996). Todorov's essay, "Living Alone Together," appears on pp. 1–14; the reply by Robert Wokler, "Todorov's Otherness," on pp. 43–55; and Todorov's response, "The Gaze and the Fray," on pp. 95–106.

by formulating this thesis explicitly," Todorov finds, "it becomes questionable—from Rousseau's own point of view" (47). Rousseau is aware of the dangers of pursuing a solitary life modeled in some ways after existence in the state of nature, "but he does not say so clearly." Rousseau's "usual intellectual vigilance" is temporarily relaxed (49). In the end, however, Rousseau "shows that the way of the solitary individual does not lead to happiness and he refrains from recommending it to us" (53).

While other readers conclude that Rousseau's pursuit of the two ways of the citizen and the solitary individual ends in confusion *or* extremism, Todorov sees a "third way" in Rousseau's thought that offers some hope. The "third way" is not a panacea, but it also does not suffer from the one-sided limitations of the other ways available to mankind. Rousseau never makes this "third way" thematic or gives it a specific name, Todorov admits, so he himself terms it the way of the "moral individual." The moral individual is, in one sense, an alternative version of the ideal of the individual, the ideal of "man" as opposed to "citizen." However, unlike the ideal "man," pursued by Rousseau to its logical conclusion in the form of the solitary individual, the moral individual is meant to live in society. The moral individual is therefore, in another sense, a middle way between the extremes of "man" and "citizen," the solitary and the patriot. The "third way" is a path of moderation that integrates and articulates some of the elements of the two more extreme ways. Todorov finds the "reconciliation of these two opposing terms—the integration of the natural ideal with social reality" (56), in Rousseau's pedagogical novel, *Emile*. "Rather than trying to 'denature' man, an effort will instead be made to adapt his nature to society as it exists, and to bring his own existence closer to the ideal" (57). The domestic education Emile receives will produce a moral individual with a humanitarian outlook. This outlook encompasses what Todorov calls "wisdom," a wisdom that consists of recognizing the existence of others as independent subjects and accepting responsibility for our actions as moral beings. "Rousseau himself did not always follow this path," Todorov notes, "and yet it is the only one he recommends without hesitation. It does not automatically lead to happiness. . . . It consists of practicing a healthy form of sociability: it is not much, perhaps, but it is all that is open to us." Rousseau's "third way" offers us a "frail happiness" (65–66).

IV.

The "third way" he first finds in his dialogue with Rousseau in *Frail Happiness* continues to play a central role in Todorov's more recent inquiries into modern humanism, and Rousseau remains a central figure in his elaboration of a critical humanism. Shortly after *Frail Happiness* appeared, Todorov published *On Human Diversity*, a major study of the conception of "us" and "them" in modern French thought, particularly during the eighteenth and nineteenth centuries. He therefore both contextualizes Rousseau's philosophical project by placing him within a larger tradition and draws upon the lessons he learned in his earlier dialogue with the thinker. In *On Human Diversity*, Todorov examines how various thinkers have understood the relationship between the concept of the unity of the human race, on the one hand, and the diversity of human populations, on the other. He wants to rescue humanism from its critics (as well as some of its defenders). *On Human Diversity* attempts to differentiate genuine humanism from a "narrow humanism" that adopts a single vision of humanity and refuses or represses alternative forms—a cause of the racism, colonialism, and totalitarianism witnessed in modern times (66–67). In contrast, true humanism is based on a recognition of a common human identity consistent with different expressions of that humanity, a common ethic that does not lead to intolerance or succumb to relativism. As Todorov declares in *On Human Diversity*, Montesquieu and Rousseau "embody, at their best, the humanist philosophy that allowed me to observe the distortion of its project during the nineteenth century" (394). They both allow for differences among various peoples without forswearing certain universal values; they both recognize that only moderate solutions—a "third way," as Todorov has called it—can be applied to the fundamental heterogeneity of collectivities and individuals. Through his critical dialogue with these figures, Todorov seeks to develop a humanism that accepts human freedom (and thus moral responsibility), allows the distinction between good and evil, pursues good with moderate hopes, and criticizes evil while cognizant of the flaws of human existence.

As in his earlier essay on Rousseau, Todorov argues in *On Human Diversity* that Rousseau is a crucial representative of a genuine and moderate humanism. "Rousseau's position . . . is inseparable from the humanist tradition," he writes, and "what is more, this tradition is inconceivable today without Rousseau's contributions" (23). Rousseau is the first thinker to conceive clearly the unity of the human race in terms of a common freedom and moral agency rather than any specific "natural" traits (21–22), according to Todorov. And Rousseau also recognizes that more than a single way is available to mankind. Returning to Rousseau's apparently irreducible choice between "man" and "citizen," the choice that he analyzes in *Frail Happiness,* Todorov again emphasizes in *On Human Diversity* that a third path is needed. "Rousseau is not at all an 'idealist' . . . : he knows perfectly well that only a compromise can meet these contradictory requirements, and he prefers lucidity to the euphoria of illusions" (184). He takes this lesson from Rousseau and applies it to modern thought in general. He therefore ends *On Human Diversity* with a reflection on a "well-tempered humanism" that recalls the conclusion to *Frail Happiness:* "Montesquieu and Rousseau may have understood better than others the complexities of human life, and they may have formulated a nobler ideal; even so, they found no panacea, no solution to all our problems. . . . The 'flaws' of individuals, like those of societies, are just as intrinsic as their greatest merits. It is thus up to each individual to try to make the best prevail over the worst. . . . Learning to live with others is a part of this wisdom" (399).

Todorov continues his exploration of the "third way" of moderate humanism in his most recent work on the thinkers of the past, *The Imperfect Garden: Humanist Thought in France (Le Jardin imparfait: La Pensée humaniste en France)*. As the subtitle to the work indicates, Todorov continues the study of humanist thought that he undertook in *On Human Diversity*. By "humanism," Todorov means, at the most fundamental level, any doctrine founded on the belief that humans must be the source and goal of all their actions. There are, Todorov observes, three essential characteristics of humanism. For the sake of clarity, he classifies them under the headings of "I," "You," and "They." The first person indicates the basic autonomy of the self: "I must be at the source of my actions." This alone is insufficient, for the "other," or second person, "must be the goal of such actions." Finally, the humanist recognizes the third person—the "they"—as "belonging to the human race," a recognition that elicits the virtue of tolerance. It is the fusion of these three elements—the independence of the self, the finality of the other, and the universality of the other*s*—that, "properly speaking, constitutes humanist thought."[26] Todorov thereby recasts the categories he first used in his study of the contact between Europe and the "other" in *The Conquest of America* and develops them through his dialogue with philosophers in the humanist tradition.

In *The Imperfect Garden,* Todorov concentrates on three thinkers—Montaigne, Rousseau, and Constant—in order to "build a model of humanist thought." While Montaigne produced the first coherent humanist doctrine, he argues, it only reached its

---

26. *Le Jardin imparfait: La Pensée humaniste en France* (Paris: B. Grasset, 1998), 48–49. For Todorov's earlier use of the "other," see the epilogue to *The Conquest of America;* see also *On Human Diversity,* xi.

full expression in Rousseau's thought (15–16). In articulating the moderate and critical humanist doctrine he derives from these thinkers, Todorov explicitly draws on his discovery in *Frail Happiness* that Rousseau offers a "third way" that addresses the complexity of human existence. In a lengthy section of *The Imperfect Garden* entitled "The Third Way," Todorov returns to the seemingly contradictory paths of "man" and "citizen" that Rousseau seems to propose and again insists that he offers a middle way. Rather than pursuing either path alone, Rousseau "integrates the contraries" and includes the natural ideal in social reality (261–65).[27] With this interpretation of Rousseau in hand, Todorov turns to the humanism he is building through his dialogue with the thinkers of the past. "The humanist position will here consist . . . not in choosing one of two terms"—such as nature or artifice, goodness or virtue, individualism or socialism—"but in transcending the choice itself" (291). The "third way" is the path of equilibrium and resolution. Again evoking his earlier work on Rousseau, Todorov argues in another section of *The Imperfect Garden*—one entitled "Frail Happiness"—that the "third way" of humanism offers a happiness limited to the human sphere and, given the imperfection of mankind, a fragile happiness (294–96).[28] The wisdom of the humanism Todorov draws from Rousseau's well and from other sources is to learn that happiness can take root only in the imperfect garden we inhabit (338).

27. See also Todorov's "La troisième voie," *La Revue Tocqueville/Tocqueville Review* 72, no. 2 (1996), 151–64.

28. Todorov's essay from 1996, "La troisième voie," ends with the following sentence: "Human life never knows anything, even at best, but a frail happiness" (164).

A NOTE ON THE TEXT

In *Frail Happiness,* Todorov quotes Rousseau's works extensively, following each passage with a parenthetical reference to its source. Here, we have maintained his system of parenthetical citation, but we have also provided references to standard English translations. Each passage from Rousseau will be identified by a short title, relevant part (e.g., chapter) if appropriate, and the page numbers of the French edition followed by the page numbers of the English edition (when such an edition is available). For the French text, we cite the standard five-volume edition of the *Œuvres complètes* (Paris: NRF-Éditions de la Pléiade, 1959–95), identified here as *O.C.* For the English translation, we use the *Collected Writings of Rousseau (C.W.),* edited by Roger D. Masters and Christopher Kelly (Hanover: Dartmouth College/University Press of New England, 1990–), in seven volumes to date. We use other standard English translations for works not included in the *Collected Writings* series; however, if no standard English version is available for a particular work, we will cite only the French edition and translate the text ourselves. Frequently cited works appear below.

Confessions	*Confessions. O.C.*, Vol. 1; *C.W.*, Vol. 5.
Dialogues	*Rousseau, Judge of Jean-Jacques: Dialogues. O.C.*, Vol. 1; *C.W.*, Vol. 1.
Emile	*Emile; or, On Education. O.C.*, Vol. 4; translated by Allan Bloom (New York: Basic Books, 1979).
Final Reply	*Final Reply. O.C.*, Vol. 3; *C. W.*, Vol. 2.
First Discourse	*Discourse on the Sciences and Arts (First Discourse). O.C.*, Vol. 3; *C.W.*, Vol. 2.
Government of Poland	*Considerations on the Government of Poland. O.C.*, Vol. 3.
Julie	*Julie, or The New Heloise. O.C.*, Vol. 2; *C.W.*, Vol. 6.
Letters to Malesherbes	*Letters to Malesherbes. O.C.*, Vol. 1; *C.W.*, Vol. 5.
Political Economy	*Discourse on Political Economy. O.C.*, Vol. 3; *C.W.*, Vol. 3.
Reveries	*The Reveries of the Solitary Walker. O.C.*, Vol. 1; translated by Charles E. Butterworth (New York: New York University Press, 1979).
Second Discourse	*Discourse on the Origin and Foundations of Inequality Among Men (Second Discourse). O.C.*, Vol. 3; *C.W.*, Vol. 3.
Social Contract	*On the Social Contract. O.C.*, Vol. 3; *C.W.*, Vol. 4.
Social Contract, First Version	*On the Social Contract*, First Version. *O.C.*, Vol. 3; *C.W.*, Vol. 4.

frail HAPPINESS

Preface

We are all confronted, at one time or another, with choices as to what sort of life we will lead. The relationships we have to ourselves, to the people around us, to institutions, to politics: all of these, at some point, can become problematic and demand our attention.

Yet we face a certain difficulty in thinking about and (even more so) in talking about these issues. The very words that designate these choices and their consequences—such words as *existence, equality, freedom, virtue, morality*, and many others—have a hollow sound, and they elude our efforts to grasp the essence of our lives. At such times, our language seems grandiloquent and vague. Rather than risk uttering such grand, empty phrases, we content ourselves with mumbling a word here or there or we simply remain silent. Nonetheless, these issues are essential to our lives and cannot be ignored.

It has always been difficult to talk about simple things, but the difficulty has varied according to time and place. Our own era has seen the divorce of everyday language, accessible to all and therefore intended for all, from specialized languages—those of philosophers, psychologists, economists, and others—languages that are addressed to professionals, and to them alone. Reading the authors of the past often seems refreshing by comparison. In reality, though, there is a double illusion at work. First of all, we read only the texts that have survived oblivion, which represent an infinitely small number of those that were written; therefore, these works are, by definition, those closest to us. Second, these texts are among the most influential for our history; their power is such that they have imposed their language on us, and what may have then been abstruse jargon has with time become our everyday vocabulary. It nonetheless remains the case that we get the impression of having something at stake when reading them. The ideas may well be complex, indeed obscure, yet the words are simple and familiar. In short, we recognize ourselves in this language.

These thoughts come to mind when I ask myself why I decided to write this book. Put off by the language of professionals, on the one hand, and by the hollow ring of grand words, on the other, I dream of a simple way of expressing what is difficult; I find it, at least at times, in certain writers of the past. Far more than many contemporary writers, they help me to reflect more clearly upon my own life. I would like to share part of the benefit I have derived from this with my reader. My goal in reading these works is neither philosophical nor literary, though I have profited from the commentaries that literary and philosophical scholars have devoted to these authors. If I were obliged to give my aim a name, I would instead call it *practical.*

Among these exceptional writers, Jean-Jacques Rousseau is perhaps neither the most attractive nor the wisest, but he is one of the most powerful. It might be said that, perhaps more so than anyone else (particularly in France), he both discovered and invented our modernity. "Discovered," because this modern society existed before he did, but it had not yet found such a penetrating interpreter. But also "invented," because he has passed down to posterity the concepts and themes that, for two hundred years, we have not ceased to examine. Reading Rousseau today, we cannot help but attribute a prophetic clairvoyance to him; his adversaries would reply, of course, that we haven't yet freed ourselves from the myths in which he has entrapped us.

Nevertheless, I confess that for a long time I felt a certain reticence with regard to Rousseau's thought. While admiring his diction—indeed, grand eloquence—I was bothered by what I took to be a certain philosophical extremism. That is, until the day that I understood that this extremism was in fact sheer intensity of thought. Rousseau is so powerful a thinker that he immediately foresees the most distant premises and ultimate consequences of each assertion, and he communicates them all to us. But this does not mean that he simply accepts everything he says. I had been misled precisely by the apparent simplicity of his language: I believed that I understood each phrase in itself and forgot to ask myself about its place in Rousseau's overall system. Once I made this discovery, my hesitations disappeared: not that I always agree with him, but I benefit from the force of his thought as I try to think through these issues myself.

The challenge we confront today, even if we avoid talking about it in this way, is the question of what ways are open to man.[1] The answer Rousseau gives is, of course, a schematization of an infinitely complex reality. In turn, I also schematize Rousseau greatly: just as he interprets and reconstructs the world around him, I interpret and reconstruct his system, leaving out much and retaining little. After this exercise, if a useful philosophical tool remains, it will once again be Rousseau's fault.[2]

1. We have retained the gender-specific "man" when translating *"homme"* in part because Rousseau consistently uses "man" in his own works, and Todorov generally follows him in this regard, although both also use terms such as "humanity" and "the human species." Rousseau often uses "man" specifically for males, though he also seems to use the word in a gender-neutral manner. Todorov clearly uses "man" in this work and elsewhere in a gender-neutral manner to refer to both men and women.

2. By speaking of Rousseau's "fault," Todorov alludes to the long tradition (beginning with commentators on the French Revolution) of viewing Rousseau as an extremist and blaming him for modern social and political revolutionary movements.

CHAPTER I

The Structure of the Doctrine

In order to understand the different solutions to the problem of the human condition as Rousseau explores them, and to situate them in relation to one another, we must first recall the broad outlines and general structure of his doctrine. To begin with, there is the well-known opposition between nature and society, an opposition that Rousseau makes his own and that becomes in his thought an opposition between the "state of nature" and the "state of society." Corresponding to these two states are two types of man, types that Rousseau variously calls "natural man" and "the man of man," or "the man of nature" and "the man of opinion," or "savage man" and "civil man," or, yet again, "the man of nature" and "the factitious and chimerical man whom our institutions and our prejudices have substituted for him" (*Dialogues,* Second Dialogue, 728/53).

Rousseau's first argument concerning this opposition, which he himself always considered to be the ultimate foundation of his system, concerns the original goodness of man. He formulates it in the debates sparked by his first publication, the *Discourse on the Sciences and Arts:* "although man is naturally good, as I believe and as I have the happiness to feel" (*Final Reply*, 80/117 n). And he affirms it to the end of his life, calling it "his great principle": "that nature made man happy and good" (*Dialogues*, Third Dialogue, 934/213).

If the "man of nature" is good, the "man of man" is not; or, as Rousseau often says, man is good, but men are evil. The men we see around us are both depraved and unhappy. The explanation for this inversion can be found only in the transition from the state of nature to the state of society. It is our institutions, our social order—in a word, society—that have produced this disastrous result.

Up to this point, Rousseau's thought is therefore allied with the many versions of the myth of the Golden Age, a nostalgia for the past that implies a critique of the present. Rousseau himself gives this impression: the Golden Age may well be treated as a chimera, he says, but only by those who renounce any ideal and whose hearts are corrupt (*Final Reply*, 80/117; *Emile*, Bk. 5, 859/474). Moreover, he is not unwilling to assimilate this myth to his own state of nature. Recalling the origins of his thought, and particularly the *First Discourse*, he still describes his revelation in these terms: "An unfortunate question from an Academy . . . showed him another universe, a true golden age, societies of simple, wise, happy men" (*Dialogues*, Second Dialogue, 828–29/131).

Without entering into any detail for the moment, we must first note that this goodness has a somewhat singular, if not paradoxical, character. For it is displayed in a world that is, according to Rousseau, ignorant of the distinction between good and evil, since man still does not have reason at his disposal. Natural man is not intentionally good; only from an external perspective—for example, from our own perspective today—can we attest to the goodness of his conduct. Hence, at other moments, a more severe Rousseau refuses to identify the state of nature with the Golden Age. "Unfelt by the stupid men of earliest times, lost to the enlightened men of later times, the happy life of the golden age was always a state foreign to the human race, either because it went unrecognized when humans could have enjoyed it or because it had been lost when humans could have known it" (*Social Contract, First Version,* Bk. 1, Chap. 2, 283/77).

But how, then, can we account for these differences between a state of nature and a state of society? The answer is that, in the first state, man is alone: not literally alone, like Adam, but not taking into account the existence of others. The *Discourse on the Origin of Inequality* (or *Second Discourse*) repeatedly tells us that he is alone, he is solitary. He does not know any "communication with his fellows" (Note 6, 199/71), he has no need for others, he is ignorant of them. In contrast, in the state of society (its very name is revealing in this regard), man is entirely determined by social ties, by his dependence on others, by communication with his fellow men. Here, he discovers the existence of others and becomes conscious of their gaze. He begins "to look at the others and to want to be looked at himself" (*Second Discourse,* 169/47); he begins to see himself through the eyes of others and to construct a "seeming" distinct from "being." Everything in man, such as we can observe him today, is due to his sociability: "Such is, in fact, the genuine cause of these differences: the savage lives within himself; the sociable man, always outside himself, knows how to live only in the opinion of others; and it is, so to speak, from their judgment alone that he draws the sentiment of his own existence" (ibid., 193/66).

The contrast between the state of nature and the state of society, and between natural man and the man of opinion, leads Rousseau in the *Second Discourse* to formulate a second, parallel opposition: that between self-love and *amour-propre.*[1] Self-love is a sentiment that savage man shares with the animals; it is little more

---

1. The distinction between "self-love" *(amour de soi)* and "amour-propre" *(amour-propre)* is central to Rousseau's thought. There is no clear English equivalent to *"amour-propre,"* but it does carry the sense of "pride," with both positive and negative connotations. *Amour-propre* might also be rendered as "vanity."

than the instinct of self-preservation. It is "the sole passion natural to man" (*Emile*, Bk. 2, 322/92), a "primitive, innate passion, which is anterior to every other and of which all others are in a sense only modifications" (ibid., Bk. 4, 491/213). This passion is comparable to natural man himself in that, ignorant of any distinction between good and evil, it is nevertheless good. In contrast, *amour-propre*, which is only characteristic of social man, consists of his situating himself in relation to others and in preferring himself to all others; it leads to hatred of others and to discontent with himself. *Amour-propre* is the source of all the vices, while self-love is the source of all the virtues.

Contrary to the popular view (but not to that of the specialists), Rousseau does not "denigrate" society and its effects on man at all. Quite the opposite: in the *Second Discourse* he tries to deduce all the present characteristics of mankind from the sole fact of social life. From it comes reason, conscience, and the moral sense; private property, inequality, and servitude, as well as all the present forms of economic life; laws, various institutions, and war; languages, technology, sciences, and arts; our sentiments and our very passions, such as we experience them in everyday life. As he says in his *Essay on the Origin of Languages:* "He who willed that man be sociable touched his finger to the axis of the globe and inclined it at an angle to the axis of the universe. With this slight movement I see the face of the earth change and the vocation of mankind decided" (Chap. 9, 401/310).

But the popular view is not incorrect when it presents Rousseau as a partisan of the state of nature and as contemptuous of the state of society. I have already observed that his description was anything but neutral; Rousseau never abstains from letting us know where he stands. "The pure state of nature is the one above all others where men would be the least wicked, the happiest, and the most numerous on earth" (Political Fragments, 475/17). In contrast, in the state of society, "we find our advantage in the detriment of our fellows" (*Second Discourse,* Note 9, 202/75). This state "inspires in all men a base inclination to harm each other" (*Second Discourse*, 175/52). How could we ever feel any sympathy for such a condition?

Rousseau shares this negative view of humanity with a number of other great critics and satirists: Hobbes, or, in France, La Rochefoucauld. Their descriptions are similar, and Rousseau knows this, but he also sees a difference that, for him, is crucial. What these other writers believe to be the nature of man (or what belongs to him in the state of nature) is, for Rousseau, merely an effect of society. On the contrary, in the state of nature men are good. "Hobbes' mistake, therefore, is not that he established the state of war among men who are independent and have become sociable, but that he supposed this state natural to the species" (*Social Contract*, First Version, Bk. 1, Chap. 2, 288/81). "The error of Hobbes and the other philosophers is to have confused natural man with men that they have before their eyes" (*Writings on the Abbé de Saint-Pierre, O.C.*, Vol. 3, 611).

We might find it absurd to imagine a "state of nature" in which mankind is stripped of all that constitutes its identity; here, man is no longer either a "reasoning animal" or even a "social animal." Yet the opposition of "state of nature"/"state of society" will be an indispensable tool for Rousseau (and, as we will see, an effective one) in his inquiry into the ways open to man.

THE REMEDY

Rousseau is, in the name of a lost ideal, certainly a severe critic of the present condition of humanity. But does this mean that he is a primitivist, a proponent of turning back the clock? Not at all. Following his discussion of the first two states of man, he adds a third, neither in the past nor in the present but rather in the future, one that gives us a direction to follow. Only there will the remedy be found that will allow us to combat the previously diagnosed illness.

Moreover, it is misleading to speak of the "past" when discussing the state of nature, and this is the first reason why a "return" is impossible. Rousseau explains this at length and quite clearly in the preface and the exordium to the *Second Discourse*. The notion of a state of nature is only a mental construct, a fiction intended to help us comprehend reality, not a simple fact. The aim Rousseau gives himself is "to know correctly a state which no longer exists, which perhaps never existed, which probably never will exist, and about which it is nevertheless necessary to have precise notions in order to judge our present state correctly" (123/13). Rousseau's exercise in deduction has nothing in common with historical scholarship. "The researches which can be undertaken concerning this subject must not be taken for historical truths, but only for hypothetical and conditional reasonings better suited to clarify the nature of things than to show their genuine origin, like those our physicists make every day concerning the formation of the world" (132–33/19).

But even supposing that a state of nature had at one time existed (or, in a more acceptable version in terms of Rousseau's thought, that a state close to his may have existed among savage peoples), going backward is not possible: once the threshold to the "state of society" is crossed, there is no turning back to the "state of nature." Rousseau was always categorical in this regard. At the beginning of his career, in the *Observations* provoked by a reply to his *First Discourse*, he writes: "Once a people has been corrupted, it has never been seen to return to virtue" (56/53). And he reiterates this conviction at the end of his career: "Human nature does not go backward" (*Dialogues*, Third Dialogue, 935/213).

No misunderstanding has plagued Rousseau's thought for so long as the project attributed to him of banishing the arts and sciences from the state. Such an effort, Rousseau declares, would be pointless: the evil has already been done. Even more grave, such an expulsion would inevitably have a negative result, for barbarism would be added to corruption. Although they are derived from the decline of man, in the present state of things, the arts and sciences serve as barriers to an even greater decline. The same applies to social life in general. "What!" he exclaims in Note 9 of the *Second Discourse*, "Must we destroy societies, annihilate thine and mine, and go back to live in forests with bears? A conclusion in the manner of my adversaries, which I prefer to anticipate rather than leave them the shame of drawing it" (207/79). Such a solution is inconceivable for society in general and unacceptable to Rousseau himself: "I feel too strongly in my own particular case how little I can forego living with men as corrupt as myself" (*Letter to Philopolis*, 235/131).

The remedy is not, therefore—and never was—a return to the "state of nature." It consists of going forward, not in retracing our steps. Rousseau conceives of a future ideal, and all his work after the *Second Discourse* is devoted to its description. Far from there being a contradiction between his later work and the *Discourse,* the two stand in a necessarily complementary relationship. The later writings provide the answer to a question formulated in the earlier one, constituting a constructive effort that follows the essentially critical analysis of the present. Moreover, we glimpsed this outcome within the *Discourse* itself: there, the State of Geneva (the recipient of the dedication) is praised, not criticized, because it is governed "in the manner most approximate to natural law and most favorable to society" (111/3). Is this possible? In this regard, Rousseau cites, again in Note 9, a positive form of social behavior: the exercise of virtue, the love of one's neighbor, obedience to the laws and to the Prince. . . . In short, our situation is not hopeless, and it is enough to take the right direction. As Rousseau writes in the first version of the *Social Contract:* "far from thinking that there is neither virtue nor happiness for us and that heaven has abandoned us without resources to the depravation of the species, let us attempt to draw from the ill itself the remedy that should cure it. Let us use new associations to correct, if possible, the defect of the general association. Let [our interlocutor] himself judge its success. Let us show him in perfected art the reparation of the ills that the beginnings of art caused to nature" (Bk. 1, Chap. 2, 288/82; see Political Fragments, 479–80/20).[2] The outline of humanity's destiny now no longer resembles the Golden Age, but rather the Christian myth, with its three stages of original innocence, fall, and redemption (a formal resemblance, to be sure, that might serve to underscore all that opposes Rousseau to Christianity). Rousseau has become an optimist.

But before entering into the details of the proposed treatment, we must face an unexpected complication. We have hardly glimpsed an escape from the impasse, and Rousseau warns us against a new danger. There is not a single remedy, and this very multiplicity itself poses a problem.

MAN AND CITIZEN

Things would have been simple if the men of today resembled the inhabitants of ancient republics such as Sparta and Rome. In that epoch, says Rousseau, the individual did not exist as an independent entity. He was only a fragment of the city: only a *citizen*. It would then be enough to find a solution to the problem of the ideal city in order for its inhabitant to become happy as well. But the situation of man today is quite otherwise. On the one hand, like the Spartan or Roman, he is a member of a particular society, a citizen held responsible for acting for its greatest good. But on the other hand, he has become an individual: a being who constitutes an autonomous entity, who depends solely upon himself for his happiness. He is also a *man* or, as Rousseau also says, a "natural man." "Natural man is entirely for himself. He is a numerical

2. The "interlocutor" to whom Rousseau refers is the so-called violent reasoner whom he imagines himself trying to convince that there is a benefit in joining society and obeying its laws. In this first version of his political treatise, Rousseau frames his discussion of the social contract as a reply to the question posed by his imagined interlocutor.

unity, the absolute whole which is relative only to itself or its kind. Civil man is only a fractional unity dependent on the denominator; his value is determined by his relation to the whole, which is the social body" (*Emile*, Bk. 1, 249/39–40).

The opposition between man and citizen cannot be assimilated to that between the state of nature and the state of society, nor to that between the man of nature and the man of society. The latter opposition describes an idealized sequence and hence an irreversible one. In the other opposition, "man" has likewise sprung up *after* "citizen," but in an entirely different sense of the word. First, it is a question of historical contingency and not of the identity of the human race. The Romans, in this regard, are different from the French, but they both belong to the class of "the man of man." Second, as is the case with the inhabitants of modern countries, the two categories can certainly coexist. In the present case, then, we are no longer crossing from one stage to another, but instead we find ourselves confronted with an alternative.

The two sets of oppositions are autonomous. Nevertheless, it is Rousseau who first introduces the confusion by calling "natural man"—for reasons that are obviously not accidental—both the purely imaginary inhabitant of the state of nature and the very real inhabitant of contemporary States. The latter, of course, lives in a social state and cannot by any stretch of the imagination be confused with the man of nature. Rousseau frequently calls him simply "man" (it ought to be noted that this concerns a being of the masculine sex), but the difference is not always so clear. So in order to avoid this confusion (and in order to put ourselves in a position to measure its effects), let's introduce a new term here, one that is foreign to Rousseau's systematic terminology but that corresponds to the entity he is trying to identify. In opposition to the citizen, we will speak of the *individual*.

The ways of the citizen and the individual do not coincide, and for very obvious reasons: their goals are not the same. The former seeks the success of the group, and the latter, that of the person.

To delineate the difference more clearly, Rousseau chooses figures who embody one path or the other, but who are equally admirable. In the *Final Reply*, the role of the citizen is played by Brutus, "having his children killed for having conspired against the State" (88/123). There, the other role is not attributed to anyone, but later, when Rousseau reconsiders Brutus, he does so in opposition to Saint Augustine's condemnation of him (Political Fragments, 506/38–39). The antithesis is developed in greater detail in the article *Political Economy*, where the individuals who embody the two poles are Cato and Socrates.[3] This choice reveals that even if the role of citizen is the particular domain of the ancients (in this case the Romans), the second role is not thereby reserved for the moderns, nor even the Christians of antiquity. The way of the individual already existed during the ancient epoch, since Socrates chose it (Rousseau's Socrates, it goes without saying). The opposition is not, as we see, between ancients and moderns, as certain formulations might lead one to suppose, but rather, at the very heart of these terms, between two divergent tendencies, illustrated by Sparta and Athens in ancient times or by Geneva and Paris in modern times. The most that one can say is that the spirit of the citizen is preponderant in the ancient epoch; that of the individual, in the modern period.

Socrates and Cato are equally admirable, but for different reasons. The former sees only men, makes no distinction between his compatriots and others, and aspires to personal virtue and wisdom. The latter, in contrast, recognizes only his fellow citizens and works on behalf of common happiness, not his own.

Rousseau returns to this distinction in his chapter of the *Social Contract* devoted to "Civil Religion." This time, it is the citizen who is not identified. The individual is no longer Socrates but

3. *Political Economy* was originally published as an article in the *Encyclopedia* edited by Diderot and d'Alembert. See *Political Economy* (255/151). See also the fragment entitled "Comparison of Socrates and Cato" (*Collected Writings*, Vol. 4, 15).

Christ, and the difference is cast in terms of "the religion of man and that of the citizen" (Bk. 4, Chap. 8, 464/219). But the substance of the terms remains the same: the former's universalism stands in contrast to the latter's patriotism. Because of this universalism, the Christian religion is incompatible with any national project: "far from attaching the citizens' hearts to the State, it detaches them from it as from all worldly things" (ibid., 465/220). "Since the Gospel does not establish a national religion, a holy war is impossible among Christians" (ibid., 467/222).

It cannot be said that one of these terms is privileged and the other is not. Instead, they reflect two independent value systems. The universality of the Christian religion has led to the separation of "the theological system from the political system" (ibid., 462/217), but this theology, having become universal, is nothing other than morality. Politics and morality cannot be confused. Here, once again, Rousseau often uses the same terms to designate distinct realities: at times he speaks of "virtue," even though *civic* virtues do not necessarily coincide with *humanitarian* virtues. Similarly, he speaks of "justice" without stating precisely whether it is exercised in relation to national laws or to universal precepts (in which case it might be called "equity").

Not satisfied with revealing the difference between these two ways open to man, Rousseau goes so far as to insist upon their radical incompatibility: they are mutually exclusive. This, at least, is what he thinks during the writing of *Emile:* "Forced to combat nature or the social institutions, one must choose between making a man or a citizen, for one cannot make both at the same time" (Bk. 1, 248/39). The success of patriotism is inversely proportionate to that of humanitarianism. "Good social institutions are those that best know how to denature man" (ibid., 249/40). Here, the word "denature" implies the "natural man" as opposed to the citizen. "The legislator who desires both [these virtues] will obtain neither of them; this harmony has never been witnessed, and it never will be, since it is contrary to nature, and since two different objects cannot be given to the same passion" (*Letters Written from the Mountain*, Letter 1, *O.C.*, Vol. 3, 706).

Rousseau was neither the first nor the last to evoke this conflict. The classic example of this is Antigone, who, like Brutus, is forced to choose between the law of the city and that of humanity. In the modern epoch, Max Weber has offered the most provocative formulation for this in his distinction between the *ethics of responsibility* and the *ethics of conviction* (tantamount to the distinction between politics and morality). But Rousseau's vision is particularly dramatic: where others see a simple divergence, he himself sees an irreducible opposition.

The situation is aggravated by the fact that Rousseau is convinced that this contradiction, as with any contradiction, is a source of irreparable unhappiness (the nostalgia sparked by the loss of unity is presented as an axiom posited without argumentation). In fact, it is the principal source of men's unhappiness: "What causes human misery is the contradiction . . . between nature and social institutions, between the man and the citizen. . . . Give him entirely to the State or leave him entirely to himself; but if you divide his heart, you tear him to pieces" (Political Fragments, 510/41). Composite beings, we can achieve neither of the two ideals; by dint of serving two masters, we are neither good for ourselves nor good for others. "Make man united and you will make him as happy as he can be" (ibid.). "To be someone, to be oneself and always one, a man must act as he speaks. . . . I am waiting to be shown this marvel so as to know whether he is a man or a citizen, or how he goes about being both at the same time" (*Emile*, Bk. 1, 250/40).

Man has a double and contradictory ideal. Yet he can be happy only as a unity. The conclusion of this syllogism follows of itself: man will always be unhappy. The discovery of this new form of misery thus extinguishes the hope we had just barely glimpsed. Each of the two envisioned ways, those of the citizen and the individual, might have helped man climb out of the unhappiness into which he was plunged by his fall into the social state. But driven to pursue both ways simultaneously and not being able to do so, he is instead condemned to misery.

TWO VERSIONS OF THE IDEAL INDIVIDUAL

We are not yet done with running through the schema that Rousseau proposes for human destiny. A final distinction must be recalled, one that is all the more important because, unlike the preceding ones, Rousseau never really makes it thematic. He does not use specific terms to designate the two branches of a new alternative, even though he describes the characteristics of each of these two ways at length. At issue are two different versions of the ideal of the individual, both of which are opposed to that of the citizen.

The opposition is, however, perceptible in the wording of a few phrases. Concerning Socrates, for example, Rousseau said both that his happiness depended solely upon himself and that his love was devoted to the entire world. Be it in the name of the isolated person or of mankind, the way of the individual is always opposed to that other ideal that puts the interests of the city above all else, but the two opposing ideals do not coincide. We have likewise seen Rousseau place civil man, who lives in a "particular society," face-to-face with "natural man," who is relative "only to himself or his kind" (*Emile*, Bk. 1, 249/39). But the use of "or" in this phrase introduces a substantial difference, especially when we consider the importance Rousseau gives in his writing to the themes of solitude and communication. At other times, the distinction is not made explicit but rather imposes itself. Thus, when he evokes the two opposed ways in *Emile*, he identifies them as "raising a man for himself" and "raising him for others" (ibid., 248/39). In this particular instance, it is the second term that is too vague, since "others" can be his fellow citizens just as well as humanity as a whole. Finally, another passage in *Emile* provides a clearer formulation: "Now that Emile has considered himself in his physical relations with other beings and in his moral relations with other men, it remains for him to consider himself in his civil relations with his fellow citizens" (Bk. 5, 833/455). These three successive perspectives on the life of a single man also correspond to three different ways and to three types of man: the isolated individual, who inhabits the body; the citizen, who inhabits the city; and the moral individual, who inhabits the world.

Now this third way, which easily risks passing unnoticed, is particularly interesting: rather than being directly opposed to either of the two others, it integrates and articulates some of their elements. And while the first two ways, each perfect in itself, nonetheless lead man to unhappiness (since one part of his being must be sacrificed), the third alone holds a promise of happiness, since it alone avoids the now-familiar dangers. An uncertain happiness, but nonetheless possible.

The distinctions that have been established up to this point might be summarized in the following schematization:

$$
\text{STATE OF NATURE} \longrightarrow \text{STATE OF SOCIETY} \longrightarrow
\begin{cases}
\text{THE CITIZEN} \\
\\
\text{THE INDIVIDUAL}
\begin{cases}
\text{PHYSICAL AND SOLITARY} \\
\\
\text{MORAL AND UNIVERSAL}
\end{cases}
\end{cases}
$$

Rousseau has amply described each of the three ways distinguished in this manner. The first is the aim of the political writings in particular, from the *First Discourse* to the *Considerations on the Government of Poland.* The second path is the one that his autobiographical writings present in detail, from the *Letters to Malesherbes* to the *Reveries.* The third is set out principally in *Emile.* It goes without saying that this division is only an approximation.

Rousseau also "defends" each of the three ways available to man. Does this mean that he contradicts himself? I do not think so. If there is a contradiction, it is in the human condition; there is nothing contradictory in the act of observing and describing a contradiction. In order to speak about each of these ways, Rousseau adopts its particular perspective. To remove the impression of any contradiction, it is enough to note that he practices a kind of "free indirect style": he may write "I," but he is speaking in the name of the citizen, or the solitary man, or the moral man—not at all the same thing. Far from reproaching him for an illusory contradiction, we should instead be grateful to him for having lent his genius to these different roles, and for thus allowing us to understand the logic of each position.

Let's now try to see what Rousseau thought about these ways open to man.

CHAPTER 2

The Citizen

CIVIC EDUCATION

The principal subject of Rousseau's political writings is not the life of the citizen, but that of the city; nevertheless, the principal characteristics of the man who inhabits it can be deduced from the ideal image of the city. The two characteristics we will examine here concern education and love of the fatherland.

Rousseau distinguishes between two sorts of education: public and private, or civic and domestic, which are meant, respectively, for the citizen and for the individual. As for public education, he is inspired by Plato—whose *Republic* he judges to be "the most beautiful educational treatise ever written" (*Emile*, Bk. 1, 250/ 40)—and wants it to be entrusted entirely to the representatives of the State. The results of public education matter more to the State than to individuals (to fathers, Rousseau says), and so the beneficiary ought to direct the development of that education. This will be one of the first tasks of a well-advised government. "The law should regulate the content, the sequence, and the form of their studies" (*Government of Poland*, Chap. 3, 966). This education should be applied to everyone in an identical manner: "Since all of them are equal under the constitution of the State, they should be raised together and in the same manner" (ibid., 967). And it should encompass the entire life of each, including what others might consider private leisure activities. "They should not be allowed to play separately each as they please, but all together and in public" (ibid., 968).

This education concerns not only public behavior or actions; it should also penetrate as far as everyone's heart of hearts, for nothing stands beyond the interest of the State. "If it is good to know how to use men as they are, it is better still to make them what one needs them to be. The most absolute authority is that which permeates to the inner man and is exerted no less on his will than on his actions" (*Political Economy*, 251/148). If, then, education is well conducted, the pupils will have learned "never to want anything except what the society wants" (ibid., 261/156).

The most effective means for attaining this goal is to insure that the State is informed of the actions and thoughts of its citizens. It is therefore essential that they never escape the State's relentless gaze. Nothing could be more logical: the distinctive characteristic of the state of nature, as has been seen, was the absence of the other's gaze. In contrast, the social state begins at the moment that each individual looks at others and wants to be looked at himself. The ideal city—which is such only because it completes a process that was only partly realized with the passage to the social state—guarantees the permanent surveillance of everyone by everyone. Such is the surest means to guarantee the well-being of the State: "It is to see to it that all the citizens constantly feel that they are under the gaze of the public" (*Government of Poland*, Chap. 12, 1019). This is more easily accomplished in small States: like villages, they have the advantage that "all the citizens know each other and know one another by sight" (ibid., Chap. 5, 970). He who is anonymous is dangerous: "My preference is that . . . an office-holder never be permitted to move about incognito" (ibid., Chap. 11, 1007).

The effect of collective education, along with the surveillance it entails, will be to homogenize the relations man has with his surrounding world. This, in turn, considerably simplifies the problems of public life. In the state of nature, man knows only a single type of relation, that to things, which are always subordinate in relation to himself: he makes use of them (to nourish himself, to protect himself, and so on). With the social state, a new type of relation is introduced, that to men. But he still maintains his relations to things, and this plurality of relations is the source of various complications. In the ideal city, however, homogeneity becomes possible once again. "If the laws of nations could, like those of nature, have an inflexibility that no human force could ever conquer, dependence on men would then become dependence on things again" (*Emile*, Bk. 2, 311/85). If the particular will is entirely subject to the general will—that is, in practice, to inflexible laws—all relations are once again unified: for each man, other men will no longer be distinguished from things. As a result, man will not have to recognize other subjects outside of himself, just as he will not be recognized as a subject by others. Men and things will have the same status for him: that of instrument and object. The very notion of an individual subject, endowed with an independent will, has no meaning from the perspective of the city (even if in other respects the city, as Rousseau conceives of it, resembles an individual subject). It is in this way that "one would unite in the Republic all the advantages of the natural state to those of the civil state" (ibid.).

The passage through the complete cycle of civic education will, in turn, legitimate another action: the State will be able to punish those who contravene its will. Since this education is obligatory for all, nobody will be able to appeal to ignorance as an excuse. In the ideal city, there will be, as a sort of final examination, a "solemn oath," by which each citizen vows to respect the ideals of the city (*Constitutional Project for Corsica*, *O.C.*, Vol. 3, 943). Those who have not yet taken the oath and who violate its principles deserve exile: "Without being able to obligate anyone to believe them, [the sovereign] can banish from the State anyone who does not believe them" (*Social Contract*, Bk. 4, Chap. 8, 468/222–23). If the person has already vowed, and has not kept his word, the punishment is more severe: "If someone who has publicly acknowledged these same dogmas behaves as though he does not believe them, he should be punished with death" (ibid.).

Such a notion of public education, with all it entails, cannot be applied to the type of State we today call democratic. Today, parents agree to send their children to public school and do not protest if this teaching has as its horizon a certain "republican virtue." Yet at the same time, they are careful to preserve the right to a complementary education, one that is domestic and their sovereign domain. For example, games belong to this latter domain, and not the former. Just as a totalitarian approach in education is rejected in quantitative terms, so too should it be in qualitative terms as well: the law sanctions actions, not thoughts. School leaves political and religious convictions alone, and does not aspire to transform and unify all wills. The inhabitant of a democracy wants to be able to enjoy the anonymity of large cities in which part of his life is lived precisely incognito. He sympathizes with dissent, or freedom of opinion, which is punished elsewhere by exile, incarceration, or death. All the criticisms addressed by the contemporary democrat to public education and its effects, such as Rousseau describes them, come back in the end to a single principle: that of individual liberty, conceived as the right of an individual to protect certain parts of his life from the control exercised by the community and its instruments. It is nearly tautological to remark that civic education favors the group that directs it. It does not care about the interests of the individual, and even positively threatens them; it clearly does not favor individual variations and personal initiative. This is the case not just for totalitarian education, but for any form of public education: the group defends the interests of the group, not those of its members. This is why the members of democratic States demand, by way of guarantee, an indication of the limit beyond which the State has no right to go, and beyond which they, as individuals, decide everything.

The inhabitant of a democratic country is therefore at odds with the principles of civic education expounded by Rousseau. Does this mean that he is in disagreement with Rousseau? In other words, does Rousseau himself assume the position of the "citizen"? This question is important: it is not a matter of knowing what Rousseau, as a private individual, thinks of this ideal, but of the status he gives to the very exposition of his ideas. His answer is clear. "Public instruction no longer exists and can no longer exist, because where there is no longer a fatherland, there can no longer be citizens" (*Emile,* Bk. 1, 250/40). A historical event occurred that irreparably separates ancient Sparta from modern France: men began to think of themselves as individuals endowed with their own wills, as subjects, as wholly separate entities, and not merely as fractional parts of the vaster entity that is the community. Yet history can be neither rewritten nor undone. If Rousseau recommends to the Poles that they institute this education, it is because he believes that Poland remains isolated from European history and is thus easily assimilated to Sparta. If a modern State wants to promote a strictly civic education, then, it will inevitably collide with the "subjective" mentality of its citizens and will be able to impose it only by force. Both of them will suffer for it.

Champion of individual freedom and of the free determination of the subject, Rousseau does not advocate civic education for his contemporaries. Instead, he presents an "if . . . then" analysis: if one assumes the perspective of the citizen, then this is what follows. Let those who are committed to this way be aware of the consequences of their actions.

PATRIOTISM AND COSMOPOLITANISM

In order to define the citizen, Rousseau appeals to the notion of the fatherland. In contrast, "man" does not want to favor his people over the rest of humanity. It is in these terms that the choice is presented. "Patriotism and humanitarianism are, for example, two virtues that are incompatible in terms of their force, especially among an entire people" (*Letters Written from the Mountain*, Letter 1, *O.C.*, Vol. 3, 706). The principal function of civic education is to inculcate patriotism. "Upon first opening his eyes, an infant should see the fatherland and he should see nothing except it until his death." A citizen is a patriot or he is nothing: "This love [of the fatherland] makes up his whole existence: he sees only the fatherland, he lives only for it. The moment he is alone, he is nothing; the moment there is no longer a fatherland, he is no more, and if he is not dead, so much the worse" (*Government of Poland*, Chap. 4, 966). It is for this reason as well that, along with the civic education meant for the young, every State should cultivate national institutions, traditional practices, customs, ceremonies, games, festivals, spectacles. The more the various forms of social life are specific to one country, and to no other, the more they help attach the citizen to his fatherland. Formed in this way, the citizen will feel that he is a Pole, or a Frenchman, or a Russian, rather than a man. And patriotism having become his "dominant passion" (ibid., Chap. 3, 964), all his values will necessarily be derived from national values. "In a word, an execrable proverb must be inverted, and every Pole must say in the depths of his heart: *Ubi patria, ibi bene*" (ibid., 963).

The counterpart for this love for all that belongs to the fatherland is a certain scorn for what does not belong to it, most notably for strangers. Such is the example of the idealized cities of antiquity: the Spartan makes equality the rule at home, but behaves iniquitously as soon as he crosses the borders of his fatherland; likewise, "the humanity of the Romans extended no further than their domination," and violence was not prohibited if directed toward foreigners (*Social Contract*, First Version, Bk. 1, Chap. 2, 287/81). Being democrats at home does not stop them from being slaveholders or colonialists abroad: such is the logic of patriotism.

"Every patriot is harsh to foreigners. They are only men. They are nothing in his eyes. This is a drawback, inevitable but not compelling. The essential thing is to be good to the people with whom one lives" (*Emile*, Bk. 1, 248–49/39). If, then, the Poles of today want to follow the example of ancient citizens, they should acquire "a natural repugnance to mixing with foreigners" (*Government of Poland*, Chap. 3, 962).

The same mistrust is found from one State to another, making autarchy an ideal for every country. "The happiest nation is the one that can most easily do without all the others" (Political Fragments, 512/42). This is why Rousseau advises the Corsicans and the Poles to avoid all dependence upon others, to watch over their freedom by not having need of anyone.

Once again, there is nothing paradoxical about this reasoning. Indeed, it is even trivial: to defend and exalt the fatherland means to prefer it to other countries (and to humanity). This is the logic (and the ethic) of the citizen. Cato is a better citizen than Socrates. But is this indeed Rousseau's opinion? In other words, does he side with patriotism or instead with "cosmopolitanism"?

Several references to cosmopolitanism are found in Rousseau's writings, and it has sometimes been thought that his attitude on this issue changed. Actually, it did not. He makes his first pronouncement on cosmopolitanism in the *Discourse on the Origin of Inequality*, where he praises "a few great cosmopolitan souls" who transcend the borders that separate countries and who "include the whole human race in their benevolence" (178/54). Subsequently, although the word "cosmopolite" is no longer used in the same sense, Rousseau maintains the same principle: virtue and justice— or, more correctly, humanitarian virtues and equity—are on the side of humanity. (The implications of this credo will be explored when we turn to the "third way" available to man.)

What, then, about the texts in which Rousseau seems to disparage cosmopolitanism? Let us reread them. In fact, he denounces "those supposed cosmopolites who, justifying their love of the fatherland by means of their love of the human race, boast of loving everyone in order to have the right to love no one" (*Social Contract*, First Version, Bk. 1, Chap. 2, 287/81). Clearly, his reprobation is directed toward pretended, not true, cosmopolites. He rises up against the gap between speech and action, a characteristic of the "philosophers" (we would say "intellectuals")[1] who hide their egoism behind broad declarations. Rousseau will later return to the same accusation, but this time the word "cosmopolite" will designate only the latter form of the love of men: "Distrust those cosmopolitans who go to great length in their books to discover duties they do not deign to fulfill around them. A philosopher loves the Tartars so as to be spared having to love his neighbors" (*Emile*, Bk. 1, 249/39). How much easier it is to defend noble causes from afar than to practice those professed virtues oneself. The love of what is distant costs the individual less than the love of what is near.

In reality, Rousseau never renounced his attachment to universalistic principles. Instead, what he has done is to take up each of the perspectives in succession, that of the citizen and that of the individual (once again, one can admire both roles), and to describe their various characteristics. When he says, with regard to scorn for foreigners, that "this is a drawback, inevitable but not compelling," it is the citizen, and not Rousseau, who speaks. When he describes universalism as a "healthy idea" (*Social Contract*, First Version, Bk. 1, Chap. 2, 287/81), it is the individual who speaks. There is no contradiction here.

Yet Rousseau goes further. He does not limit himself to presenting two systems of equally coherent values so that one might choose arbitrarily between them; he also investigates their internal hierarchy. And he concludes that one must place man above citi-

---

1. "Philosophers" is a translation of *"philosophes."* The term means not only "philosophers" in a generic sense but also refers to a group of writers and thinkers, especially those associated with the *Encyclopedia*, who were the prototype of the modern intellectual or the "public intellectual."

zen. "Let us first seek this religion and this morality, and it will be that of all men; and then, when national formulas are necessary, we shall examine their foundations, relations, appropriateness, and after having said what a man is, we will then say what a citizen is" (*Letter to Beaumont, O.C.,* Vol. 4, 969). Man precedes citizen: such is the order of reason. This does not, however, prevent the order from being reversed: "we do not really begin to become men until after we have been Citizens" (*Social Contract,* First Version, Bk. 1, Chap. 2, 287/81). One is born in a particular country, and it is only through an act of will that one becomes a man, that is, a citizen of the world. Rousseau is still more direct in one of his autobiographical writings: "In general, every party man, by that alone an enemy of the truth, will always hate [Jean-Jacques]. . . . there is never any disinterested love of justice in these collective bodies. Nature engraved it only in the hearts of individuals" (*Dialogues,* Third Dialogue, 965/237 n).

What, then, is the inherent defect of patriotism? In preferring one part of humanity to the rest, the citizen transgresses a fundamental principle, that of equality. Without explicitly saying it, he accepts the notion that men are not equal. Moreover, the Spartan narrows his sense of equality in the interior of the city itself, since he excludes slaves and women from it. In Poland, too—a modern Sparta—everything that makes one effeminate will be avoided. But true morality, true justice, true virtue all presuppose equality.

Public-spiritedness, the way of the citizen, is therefore defined by a twofold opposition. On the one hand, it does not show any consideration for the interests of the individual and endangers the principle of freedom. On the other hand, it carries us away from humanity, and it revokes the principle of equality. Rousseau does not condemn it in itself, however. Within certain limits, it is commendable: if we cherish the values of our fatherland, we must be ready to defend those values, even if that means giving our lives. Furthermore, the concern for the common good must serve as a brake on the egoistic appetites of each person. Rousseau's teaching is presented as a theorem: any action benefiting the life of the community potentially harms the interests of the person as a human being (insofar as what it entails infringes on his freedom) and harms the interests of mankind (insofar as it eliminates the principle of liberty). We might choose to take this path, but we must then be prepared to make the sacrifice. Rousseau clearly sees that one choice is preferable, and he does not conceal his judgment on this point, even if he refrains from imposing it on us. The refusal to recognize the equality of men amounts to a return to a primitive (pre-Christian) barbarism. The failure to protect man's freedom amounts to a refusal to recognize that we do not live today as we did in times of old. It is tantamount to practicing a form of intolerance that has long been intolerable.

CHAPTER 3

The Solitary Individual

SOLITUDE

The citizen must identify with the group, while the individual must lead his life in solitude: this is the first version of his ideal.

The theme of solitude has many facets in Rousseau's writing. We might begin with an admission he makes, followed by regret: he is alone in the world, even though he would have liked to have been with others. "I was born for friendship" (*Confessions*, Bk. 8, 362/304); I was "the most sociable and the most loving of humans" (*Reveries*, First Walk, 995). Yet he finds himself alone, and thus unhappy. It is a "very great misfortune" (*Confessions*, Bk. 8, 362/304), and he dreads "the horror of this solitude" (*Dialogues*, Third Dialogue, 976/245), which he finds "awful" (ibid., First Dialogue, 713/42). It would therefore seem that he might nourish a hope of rejoining society: "We can give him back in his old age the sweetness of true society, which he lost so long ago and which he no longer hoped to find again here below" (ibid., Third Dialogue, 950/225). The cause of this solitude is therefore not within him, but is instead due either to the hostile attitude of others or to the fact that they are unworthy of his love. "He who ought to answer me has yet to arrive" ("My Portrait," *O.C.*, Vol. 1, 1124). "It is less my fault than theirs" (*Confessions*, Bk. 5, 188/158). "He flees men only after searching among them in vain for what he should love" (*Dialogues*, Second Dialogue, 824/127).

This, however, is not the end of the matter. Rousseau also at times associates suffering in solitude with a refusal to end it: herein lies the distinction between authentic and superficial communication. The latter does not cure solitude. To the contrary: it is in the company of others that one suffers solitude even more intensely. So Saint-Preux describes his arrival in Paris: "I enter with a secret horror into this vast desert of the world. This chaos presents me with nothing but horrible solitude, wherein reigns a dull silence. . . . 'I am never less alone than when I am alone,' said an ancient, I on the other hand am alone only in the crowd" (*Julie*, Bk. 2, Letter 14, 231/190).[1] Solitude is always deplorable, but its worst form is living in the midst of a crowd: the world is a desert, and worldly chatter, an oppressive silence. The reciprocal case is equally true: as Cicero remarked, superficial solitude, which is purely physical, is in reality authentic communication.

Thanks to this distinction between the two levels that lie at the heart of each of these attitudes, Rousseau can reconcile his nostalgia for society with his condemnation of it. This condemnation has a familiar ring: in opposition to "healthy solitude," society is replete with all the vices that characterize the "social state." This state emphasizes "seeming" to the detriment of "being," public opinion over self-esteem, vanity but not simplicity. Social institutions degrade man. Since the interior is preferable to the exterior, solitary man is superior to social man.

Communal life has a defect that is consubstantial with it: it creates a situation in which one being is dependent upon another, which therefore diminishes our freedom. Yet freedom is the individual's ideal. This, at least, is how Rousseau sees himself: "the

---

1. Scipio Africanus is quoted thus by Cicero, *De Officiis* III.1.

cause of this invincible disgust I have always experienced in the company of men . . . is nothing other than that indomitable spirit of freedom which nothing has been able to overcome" (*Letters to Malesherbes*, Letter 1, 1132/573). Let there be no mistake on this score: here, too, we must distinguish between apparent and authentic freedom. He who believes himself free is very often the slave of men, since he depends upon their opinion; the prisoner, in contrast, is free because he is alone. "I have thought a hundred times that I would not have lived too unhappily at the Bastille, since I would not be restricted to anything at all except to staying there" (ibid.). Rousseau feels a "mortal aversion for all subjugation" (*Confessions*, Bk. 3, 115/96–97). He is incapable of half-measures: "If I begin to be enslaved to opinion in something, I will soon be enslaved to it in everything all over again" (ibid., Bk. 8, 378/317). As a result, it is better to seek refuge in radical solitude. Is this not one of the reasons that he abandoned his children—the fear of dependents? The noxious character of communal life is also transposed to the physical plane: "Man's breath is deadly to his kind. This is no less true in the literal sense than the figurative. Cities are the abyss of the human species" (*Emile*, Bk. 1, 277/59).

Society is bad, solitude is good: the solitary man has no real need of others, for he is a self-sufficient being. Does not Epictetus teach us that true goods are those we find within ourselves? Does not Montaigne advise us to stop borrowing from others, and instead delve within ourselves? The man who "knows how to enjoy his own being" (*Julie*, Bk. 4, Letter 11, 482/396) cannot be praised too much. In the Stoic tradition to which Rousseau here lays claim, we find the ideal depicted under the name of the "state of nature," since it was defined precisely as men's self-sufficiency. This is why Rousseau can call the solitary individual "natural man."

In the preface to *Natural Son*, Diderot wrote: "It is only the evil man who is alone." Rousseau thought this remark was directed at himself, and he was deeply wounded.[2] He repeatedly offered a counterargument: in order to be evil, victims are needed, and so one must live in society, not in isolation. If I am alone I cannot harm others even if I so wished, and I am for that very reason good (see *Emile*, Bk. 2, 341/105; *Confessions*, Bk. 9, 455/382–83; *Dialogues*, Second Dialogue, 824/126–27). Perhaps sensing that this argument is rather mechanical, he takes a different tack: it is not only because it is impossible for them to harm others that solitary men are good, but because, thirsty for contact with others, they are also "naturally humane, hospitable, tender" (*Dialogues*, Second Dialogue, 789/99). Solitude is therefore good both because it is and is not what it seems. It is far from the crowd and from superficial contacts that "the truly sociable man" lives (ibid., 790/100). Yet "he who suffices unto himself does not want to harm anyone at all" (ibid.)! Each of these arguments might be valid in itself, but by placing them side by side, Rousseau renders them both dubious and reveals how much he takes to heart the defense of the solitary ideal.

This is how, through a series of distinctions and shifts, solitude is no longer a state to be dreaded but an ideal to which one can aspire: it has become "dear solitude" ("The Art of Enjoyment," *O.C.*, Vol. 1, 1173). This, in any case, is what Rousseau affirms. We might nevertheless doubt his lucidity (though not his sincerity) when we realize how often he returns to this declaration. From one end to the other of his autobiographical writings he assures his readers that he has no need of others, is happier without them, and is grateful for their hostility, for they have revealed to him unsuspected treasures within himself. "I am a hundred times happier in my solitude than I could ever be living among them" (*Reveries*, First Walk, 998/4). But if this is true, why does he repeat it so often? Far from authenticating the message, its very repetition makes it suspect; each new occurrence of the phrase reveals that

---

2. See *Confessions*, Bk. 9, 455/382–83; *Dialogues*, Second Dialogue, 789/99.

the preceding one was not quite correct. Not to mention, of course, that these very affirmations appear in books meant to be read by readers who are themselves nevertheless "others." Rousseau tells them over and over that he does not want to speak to them, so they have the right to be skeptical when he assures them, referring to himself: "as soon as he is alone he is happy" (*Dialogues*, Second Dialogue, 816/121).

LIMITED COMMUNICATION

Apart from the doubts we might entertain concerning the reality of the happiness Rousseau experiences when he is alone (and thus the subjective value of this state), an even more radical question arises concerning its very possibility: can one truly live alone? And if so, at what price? This new question becomes all the more critical as the reader quickly realizes that Rousseau does not lead the life of a hermit but instead enjoys the company of other human beings. "Solitude" must, then, not be understood literally; instead, rather than living absolutely alone, the individual must adapt to some interaction with others. Rather than solitude, it would be better to speak of "limited communication," observing the different ways in which this limitation works. These forms of limited communication might be grouped into four different categories.

1. Writing. The first transformation in the relationship with others consists of acting upon the character of the contact, substituting a mediated exchange for the intimacy of human presence. Our love is more intense when we are far from our beloved, and the other's absence not only makes us more desirable, but more at ease: Rousseau is familiar with "that need for leaving her in order to love her more" (*Confessions*, Bk. 5, 181/153). He often describes a fear that borders on panic when he thinks he has to speak to his neighbors: "This was the most inconvenient and the most dangerous of all the difficulties" (ibid., Bk. 5, 202). "That is an unbearable torture to me" (ibid., Bk. 12, 601/503). The scenes evoked by Rousseau justify the feeling of unease he describes, but the virulence of his wording is surprising. On the other hand, writing brings together all the advantages: Rousseau acknowledges that he is "a man who left his mistress in order to write her" (ibid., Bk. 5, 181/153). He is most at ease when he remains in contact with others without having to see or touch them. This preference applies not only to relations with lovers; when describing a moment of open hostility, for example, Rousseau declares, "What a fortunate occurrence and what a triumph for me if I had known how to speak, and if I had had, so to speak, my pen in my mouth?" (ibid., Bk. 12, 625/524). The most eloquent of writers, Rousseau is a pitiful speaker. As he knows all too well, his was the eloquence of the timid. He could "write with strength, although he spoke feebly" (*Dialogues,* Second Dialogue, 802/109). He always contrasts the "embarrassment of speaking" with the "pleasure of writing" (*Reveries,* Fourth Walk, 1038/57).

2. *The imaginary.* In this second case, the change no longer concerns the relationship but rather its object; the real is replaced by the imaginary, since the latter is preferable to the former. As Julie says in *The New Heloise,* "The land of illusions is, on this earth, the only one worth living in, and such is the void of things human that, with the exception of the Being who exists in himself, the only beauty to be found is in things that are not" (Bk. 6, Letter 8, 693/569; see also *Emile,* Bk. 5, 821/446). The imaginary follows immediately after God, the best incarnation of self-sufficiency. Rousseau shares this opinion and tries to put it into practice: "I find my advantage better with the chimerical beings that I assemble around me than with the ones I see in the world" (*Letters to Malesherbes,* Letter 1, 1131/572). Why this preference for "sweet illusions" (*Confessions,* Bk. 4, 158)? They are both invulnerable and flexible. Human beings hold no power over my imaginary objects ("nothing can take [the goods] of the imagination away from whoever knows how to enjoy them" [*Dialogues,* Second Dia-

logue, 814/119]), whereas I can always adjust the company of my friends to my own tastes: "I could cultivate it without effort, without risk, and always find it reliable and as I needed it to be" (*Letters to Malesherbes*, Letter 2, 1135/575). All in all, this is a fairly economical means for leading a life of self-sufficiency: one still tastes enjoyment by oneself, but only through interposed "illusions."

3. Nature. The third readjustment of human communication preserves the actual character of its object—but puts the inanimate in the place of the animate. Rousseau writes: "But, finally, what did I enjoy when I was alone? Myself, the whole universe" (*Letters to Malesherbes*, Letter 3, 1138/577). The formula seems to be open to everything, but it actually entails a substantial exclusion: men. We know that Rousseau knows how to enjoy his own company, to which he adds the universe, but without distinguishing human beings from the surrounding world. Or rather, he will make the distinction, but only to exclude them: "My first wish when I saw a fine day beginning was that neither letters nor visits might come to disturb its charm" (ibid., 1139/578). And when he finds a patch of wild forest, what he rejoices over is that "no tiresome person might come to put himself between nature and me" (ibid., 1140/578). In this relationship, the subject is the sole human being, and the object is silent nature; other men appear only as unwanted troublemakers, potential obstacles to communion with nature.

Nature reappears here, but it clearly does so in a different sense: it is the realm of the nonhuman. In his heart of hearts, Rousseau prefers plants to everything else: the mineral kingdom is not alive enough, and in the animal world, there is already too much willfulness. Disappointed by men, Rousseau will turn to collecting plants. He recommends this practice to everyone, on the condition that they do not work toward a practical end, turning plants into a simple means to another end. He is distressed to see that "All of these charming and graceful structures barely interest anyone who only wants to grind them all up in a mortar" (*Reveries*, Seventh

Walk, 1064/93–94). Rousseau's own interest does not extend beyond the plants themselves, and he tastes the pure "charm of admiration" (ibid., 1069/98).

The pleasure in communicating with plants is certain, but its importance must perhaps not be exaggerated, at least if we judge it by another observation Rousseau makes about himself: "the contemplation of nature always had a great attraction to his heart. He found in it a supplement to the attachments he needed. But he would have given up the supplement for the thing itself if he had had the choice, and he did not confine himself to talking with plants until his efforts to talk to humans proved vain. I will gladly leave the society of plants, he told me, for that of men at the first hope of finding it again" (*Dialogues,* Second Dialogue, 794/103). So, the precarious happiness of the supplement: we experience some relief in seeing that Rousseau prefers men to plants.

4. Depersonalization. Yet one cannot really live with plants alone, or with imaginary or absent beings—unless one is a hermit, one also necessarily mixes with other living people. But even here Rousseau makes those people undergo a treatment that transforms them into nonpersons. For example, he takes pride in preferring the company of the peasants at Montmorency to that of Parisian academics; the latter can talk with him, while the former only know how to ask his advice. Likewise, the Ninth Walk in the *Reveries* recounts the pleasure he finds in the company of children, but there again it is not a reciprocal relationship. All he wants from them is a "look of benevolence," which he otherwise would have to seek among animals (1089/126). Still, a person becomes such only through what distinguishes him from the beasts. In short, Rousseau accepts the presence of others on the condition that they are not subjects like himself, that they do not personalize themselves. "Even association with them could please me as long as I were a complete stranger to them" (*Reveries,* Sixth Walk, 1057/54–55). "It must be confessed, however, that I still feel pleasure in living in the midst of men as long as my face is unknown to them" (ibid., Ninth Walk, 1095/132).

Yet there is at least one person who remains constantly at his side, one who is not unknown to him—his companion, and later his wife, Therese. How can he still speak of solitude? Rousseau explains this paradox in the *Confessions*. His ideal would have been a perfect fusion with the other. "The first of my needs, the greatest, the strongest, the most inextinguishable, was entirely in my heart: it was the need for an intimate society and as intimate as it could be; it was above all for this that I needed a woman rather than a man, a lover rather than a friend. This peculiar need was such that the closest union of bodies could not even be enough for it: I would have needed two souls in the same body; since I did not have that, I have always felt some void" (Bk. 9, 414/348).

There is a classical image of friendship, especially lively in the Stoic tradition, that presents this ideal as a fusion of souls. Crying over the death of his best friend, Saint Augustine describes their relationship in this way: "As for me, I felt that my soul and his were just one soul in two bodies" (*Confessions,* Bk. 4, Chap. 6). Montaigne praised the universal mixing of souls and fusion of beings. Rousseau adopts this same image but gives it a paradoxical twist: he does not seek one soul in two bodies, but two souls in the same body. What he desires is impossible—physical fusion. A woman is differentiated in this regard from a man (and love from friendship) only because she allows closer, sexual contact (with a heterosexual man); apart from this, there is neither specificity nor any particular interest. As Saint-Preux remarks in *Julie, or The New Heloise:* "Too intimate relations between the sexes never led to anything but trouble" (Bk. 4, Letter 10, 449/369–70).

The best relationship with the other, then, is the other's absorption—which also means his disappearance. Rousseau makes use of this image on another occasion: "For to read while eating has always been my whim for lack of a tête-à-tête. It is the compensation for the society I lack. I alternately devour a page and a bite: it is as if my book was dining with me" (*Confessions*, Bk. 6, 269/225). Like plants, books serve as a substitute for friends; moreover, they become part of a series of pastries. Do friends face the same fate? Although it takes the opposite path, fusion leads to the same result as the non-acknowledgment of the other—namely, that the other no longer exists as an independent subject. Rather than fading undifferentiated into the world, the other is no longer anything but a part of me.

But let us return to Therese. It is not being devoured that threatens her, for the attempt at (corporeal) fusion, not surprisingly, fails: "whatever method I might use, we have always continued to be two" (*Confessions*, Bk. 9, 415/349). Yet, as we have seen, for Rousseau, the absence of unity leads to the presence of emptiness: a false communication and a very real solitude. The knowledge that Therese exists apart from him, that she has relationships with people other than himself (for example, with her own mother), means that he can no longer consider her as a candidate for fusion. As a result, he loses all interest in her: "the mere idea that I was not everything to her made it so that she was almost nothing to me" (ibid., 424/357). A Therese who participates in many relationships is a Therese who does not disappear within him, who does not break his solitude. This is why he can speak of "enjoying my solitude with my good Therese and her mother" (ibid., 412/346).

Therese remains by his side, but she does not disappear inside him, and she can no longer be an autonomous subject, an interlocutor, a "you." She can only occupy a subordinate position, reduced (at least in Rousseau's eyes) to a dependent existence: "What I had done for [her] I had done for myself" (ibid., Bk. 9, 419/352). She is relegated to the same status as books and plants: "In Therese I found the supplement I needed" (ibid., Bk. 7, 332/278). Of course, Rousseau rejects any attempt to see plants instrumentally, to see them solely in the context of how they might serve us. But he does not feel a similar scruple concerning

Therese, whom he presents in the *Confessions* and in his actual life as merely his auxiliary or supplement: he never allows her to speak for herself. What can be more eloquent in this regard than his evocation of his various pleasures? "They are those of my retirement, they are my solitary walks, they are those quickly passing but delightful days that I have passed entirely alone with myself, with my good and simple housekeeper, my well-loved dog, my old cat, the birds of the country, and the does of the forest, with all of nature and its inconceivable author" (*Letters to Malesherbes*, Letter 3, 1139/578). Therese is reduced to the mere function of "my housekeeper" and leads the list of pets and domestic animals. A simple element of nature, Therese serves as a bridge between "the solitary self" and God.

The example of Therese (and there are others) illustrates a significant variation on limited communication, because it reveals the truth about relationships with real persons: they tend to transform the other into a nonperson, an object or instrument. In order to live in solitude, Rousseau must refuse to give others the same status that he claims for himself. In other words, the price of solitude is the acceptance of inequality among human beings.

This series of restrictions applied to communication delineates the typical activity of the solitary man. Let's consider the first two variations: he who prefers the imaginary to the real, and writing to speaking, is clearly a writer. But what form does his writing take? Not the novel, though it is true that Rousseau wrote one. It is not an accident if modern readers look in that work for the ideas and passions of Rousseau, and not the inner lives of his characters, for their autonomy is minimal. But the novel—the true novel—is based upon the recognition of multiple subjectivities. Rousseau is aware of this point: in his "Conversation About Novels," which is meant to serve as the preface to *Julie, or The New Heloise,* he observes: "Writings intended for solitary folk must speak the language of solitary folk" (22/15). This means that in place of the original plurality of the novel, one must substitute a unity of tone, style, and characters: "everyone who comes near her is bound to resemble her; everyone about her is bound to become Julie; all of their friends are bound to have the same voice" (28/21).

The solitary will not, therefore, write novels. His works should share certain traits with the novel: private individuals, and not the collectivity or personified abstract notions, will be taken as heroes. Events will be recounted not in order to draw a lesson but in order to savor them in their singularity. And here, the two other restrictions on communication come to help us: the solitary will choose a genre in which "others" are present only to the degree that they are necessary to the subject who speaks and who narrates, and their deficiency will be supplemented by the description of nature. It is now clear: the genre in question is autobiography, whose modern form was invented by Rousseau. He requires inequality of treatment between others and himself; as he writes at the beginning of the *Confessions,* "I feel my heart and I know men" (Bk. 1, 5/5). Everything is an object for knowledge, while the "I" is the sole subject. He also requires valorization of the interior rather than the exterior. So he describes his project: "I am writing less the story of these events than that of the state of my soul as they happened" (Fragments of the *Confessions,* 1150/586). Whereas writing political treatises is not at all a citizen's duty, writing an autobiography is an entirely natural, almost inevitable, action for the solitary individual. The last fifteen years of Rousseau's life therefore merges with the autobiographical act. He notices this himself: "If I continue it, my book will by its nature end when I approach the end of my life" (Fragments of the *Reveries, O.C.,* Vol. 1, 1165). But is this end anything other than the end of the book?

For autobiography, sincerity is an essential quality, whatever the content of what one is going to say may be. In other words, reference to transcendent values is eliminated by a limitless subjectivity. "If this feeling is in me, why should I hide it? . . . Men who speak sincerely about themselves should not be corrected" ("My Portrait," *O.C.,* Vol. 1, 1122). The *Confessions* often recounts the intrinsic pleasure that the autobiographer finds in the act of speaking to himself—and still more in writing to himself. This is why Rousseau devotes himself to the activity of the autobiographer. "I like to talk about myself too much" (*Letters to Malesherbes,* Letter 3, 1142/580). It is the self-sufficient act *par excellence:* "I have enjoyed speaking to myself; I still enjoy doing so" ("The Art of Enjoyment," *O.C.,* Vol. 1, 1174). The *other* is no more fortunate as a reader than he was as a character: "I know very well that the reader does not have a great need to know all this; but I myself have a need to tell it to him" (*Confessions,* Bk. 1, 21/18).

Such, at least, is the official agenda of the genre. Rousseau often acts as though the sole rule of autobiography was the very one that present-day psychoanalysts impose on their patients: to say everything. "I will say everything: good, bad, in sum, everything" (Fragments of the *Confessions,* 1153/588). "Here is the only portrait of a man, painted exactly according to nature and in all its truth" (*Confessions,* Preamble, 3/3), "showing myself completely to the public" (*Confessions,* Bk. 2, 59/50). The language of autobiography aims at transparency, at being a pure mediator of the totality of experience, which would, as it were, fill a book. Rousseau nevertheless knows that to say everything is impossible, for that which is lived is inexhaustible. He also knows that he must choose one language among others, for the words do not impose themselves: there is no natural language. "For what I have to say it would be necessary to invent a language as new as my project: for what tone, what style does one adopt?" (Fragments of the *Confessions,* 1153/588). When he so chooses, Rousseau insightfully identifies the characteristics of the genre: "By abandoning myself at the same time both to the remembrance of the received impression and to the present feeling, I will depict the state of my soul doubly, namely at the moment when the event happened and at the moment when I described it; my style . . . will itself form a part of my story" (ibid., 1154/589). But these "professional" remarks betray a concern for the reader and a sensitivity to form that no longer correspond to the simple project of saying everything.

In the abandoned preface to the *Confessions*, Rousseau reproaches Montaigne for not adhering to this single rule: "Montaigne paints himself in a good likeness but in profile" (Fragments of the *Confessions*, 1150/586). Reflecting at a distance on his own *Confessions*, he admits that there was as much imagination as truth in the work, that he embellished one moment and omitted another, that he adhered to verisimilitude and not to truth: "I spoke of things I had forgotten as it seemed to me that they must have been" (*Reveries*, Fourth Walk, 1035/55). He therefore humbly admits that he did not necessarily do better than Montaigne: "If, without thinking about it and by an involuntary movement, I sometimes hid my deformed side and painted myself in profile . . ." (ibid., 1036/55 [trans. altered]). Is it not true that every portrait is always in profile?

Autobiography can no more adhere to the rule of saying everything than it can be concerned solely with the "I" of the narrator: the autobiographical act remains a language act that is always addressed to the "other." While the solitary individual does not truly live alone, he can treat others as though they did not exist or can refuse to recognize them. The autobiographer, the ultimate avatar of this individual, can no longer remain contented with speaking to himself: it is literature, after all, and he does address himself to others. He can flaunt his project and pride himself on carrying it out. A certain bad faith is therefore inherent in the very genre of modern autobiography (such as it was conceived by Rousseau), not merely in some of its specific manifestations.

THE QUEST FOR THE SELF

Even solitude is not sufficient, though: at best, it allows us to shut out only those who exist outside us. But the individual "I" possesses, in its interior, many ingredients that are not its own. If, then, solitude is one's ideal, this "I" must be submitted to an analysis that removes every foreign element and leaves only what belongs to itself. Let's call this remainder the *self*. Such is the experience Rousseau reports in his last work, *Reveries of the Solitary Walker.*

To begin with, others must be put at a distance, not only from one's life but also from one's being. To imagine that solitude itself suffices to free oneself from others is in effect to forget that, by passing through the social state, man has seen self-love—an autonomous passion—turn into *amour-propre,* a relative passion and itself the source of all the other passions. With the advent of *amour-propre,* "others" are found within the self, and this is the root of all our ills: it "is not in the beings who are alien to us, but in ourselves; and that is where we must exert ourselves to extract it completely" (*Reveries,* Eighth Walk, 1078/115). Such is the test to which we must subject ourselves; such is the price we must pay if we want "natural man," the solitary individual's ideal, to become synonymous with "the man of nature," that is, such as he exists before society.

This is Rousseau's new inspiration: that "I am fully myself and for myself without diversion, without obstacle" (ibid., Second Walk, 1002/12). He therefore multiplies solipsistic formulations: "I enjoy myself" (ibid., Eighth Walk, 1084/120), "I had ensnared myself on my own" (ibid., Fifth Walk, 1042/64), "I feed, it is true, on my own substance, but it is not depleted. And I am sufficient unto myself" (ibid., Eighth Walk, 1075/111). This text is not intended to dispel misunderstandings, to exonerate its author, or to set his image aright: in short, it is not addressed to others, as were the *Confessions* and the *Dialogues* (*Rousseau, Judge of Jean-Jacques*). Instead, from now on it is a matter of "conversing with my soul" (*Reveries,* First Walk, 999/5). The difference from Montaigne, momentarily lost, now reemerges: "My enterprise is the same as Montaigne's, but my goal is the complete opposite of his: he wrote

his Essays only for others, and I write my reveries only for myself"
(ibid., 1001/7).

First we shun other living people and thereby obtain solitude.
Then we eliminate interiorized others, and *amour-propre* becomes
self-love once again. But even this is not enough. Now we must
liberate ourselves from the influence of the objects that surround
us, and therefore from what ties us to them: sensation. Rousseau
knows the pleasure of contemplation, which leads him to identify
with the objects he perceives, to merge himself with the "system of
beings" (*Reveries,* Seventh Walk, 1066/95). But these moments of
ecstasy still make us too dependent upon the exterior world; we
must suppress contemplation and eliminate objects. Even fleeting
impressions must be effaced in order to enter into a new state that
he calls "reverie." "I forgot botany and plants. . . . and I began to
dream more at ease" (ibid., 1071/100).

To attain a state of reverie, a genuine apprenticeship is required: it entails a certain technique that properly orients the body
and the mind. The ideal conditions are obtained when we are
equally distant from absolute repose and rapid movement. What is
most suitable is "a uniform and moderated movement having neither jolts nor lapses" (*Reveries,* Fifth Walk, 1047/69). He therefore
suggests a boat adrift, rocked by the ebb and flow. Walking leads
to the same result, though to a lesser degree, and so too does
evoking earlier reveries. "In wanting to recall so many sweet reveries, instead of describing them, I fell back into them. This is a
state which is brought back by memory" (ibid., Second Walk,
1003/13).

But what do we discover once exterior as well as interior others
are removed, and once the sensation of objects is muted? What is
the nature of that part of the "I" that is most my own? In the
depths of being, we find the sentiment of existence. We see this
most clearly in the Fifth Walk of the *Reveries.* It is a state of
repose and tranquillity, a timeless state that is best described by
the enumeration of what it is not: neither duration nor succession,

neither pleasure nor pain, neither desire nor fear, neither objects nor sensations. Having thus created a void, the subject finds that he is replete, that his happiness "leaves the soul no emptiness it might feel a need to fill" (ibid., Fifth Walk, 1046/69). "What do we enjoy in such a situation? Nothing external to ourselves, nothing if not ourselves and our own existence. As long as this state lasts, we are sufficient unto ourselves, like God" (ibid., 1047/69).

Here the quest reaches its goal. After having eliminated everything, by a remarkable labor of subtraction and introspection, man plumbs his depths. But these depths are, strictly speaking, nothing; the subject coincides with the predicate in a perfect tautology. The self is precisely the very existence of that self—nothing more. We thereby attain repose and peace. Rousseau, more intensely than "any other man," sought "the nature and the destination of [his] being" (ibid., Third Walk, 1012/28); he ends up discovering that his nature consists precisely of searching for himself. The destination is the journey itself. So the quest becomes intransitive and is transformed into reverie; the self-sufficient man is similar to God, but his existence is now equivalent to nonexistence, to radical repose. Now, nothing separates him from death.

AN UNHAPPY END

Such, then, is the second way open to man: in order to recover from the fall into which the social state has plunged him, man should embrace the ideal of solitude. But, by formulating this thesis explicitly, it becomes questionable—from Rousseau's own point of view. (We might ask, as Rousseau's critics certainly did, if a "state of nature" in which man was stripped of his constitutive characteristic—sociality—was a proper mental construct. But, after all, this abstraction simply allowed Rousseau to formulate and organize his ideas.) Things change radically when we move away from the question of the ideal and situate ourselves in the near future, no longer in the mythical past. Recall that, according to

Rousseau himself, men have all entered into the social state and that going backward is impossible. How, then, can solitude be erected as an ideal along with its corollary, the suppression of society?

Rousseau is well aware of this difficulty, but he does not say so clearly. It is sometimes asked whether he does not cultivate confusion by refusing to admit to this inconsistency. How do we otherwise explain the fact that he calls two such very different entities as the man of the past and the man of the future, even if the latter is modeled on the former, by one name: "natural man"? His desire to maintain the parallel prevails over that for clarity. A comparable ambiguity stamps the word "society" and its derivative terms. Although this word is contained in two autonomous oppositions, "nature/society" and "solitude/society," Rousseau acts as if the same sense of the word pertained in both cases. He can therefore charge "society-contrary-to-solitude" with all the ills that characterize "society-contrary-to-nature." It is nevertheless clear that, from Rousseau's own perspective, solitude and its antithesis, society, *both* follow the fall into the social state and stand outside the state of nature. Consequently, society is unjustly condemned for what its opposite, solitude, likewise suffers.

"Nature" itself does not always remain identical to itself. And, as far as we are concerned, *nature* in the sense of "origin" appears to be linked to *nature* in the sense of "wilderness." When, in the *Confessions,* Rousseau evokes how he conceived the *Discourse on Inequality,* he shows us the connection as it unfolds: "All the rest of the day, deep in the forest, I sought, I found the image of first times whose history I proudly traced" (Bk. 8, 388/326). The state of nature is therefore portrayed in accordance with his own experience in the forest, and the aptly-named man of the woods is able to take part in both realms. "Nature as wilderness" initially lends certain of its traits to "nature as origin." So much more easily, then, can Rousseau later find the dreamt-of origin in the real forest and identify the imaginary "man of nature" with the solitary sylvan walker, the amateur herbalist.

It is inconceivable that so intense and rigorous a thinker as Rousseau could be taken in by these homonyms and ambiguities. In order for him to transmit them in his writings, a motif powerful enough to overpower his usual intellectual vigilance was required. Such a motif indeed exists, one perfectly suited to blind, temporarily, whoever comes under its sway: namely, that during the autobiographical period of his life, Rousseau decided that the solitary individual, the ideal opposed to the citizen, was himself. He explains this at length in the *Dialogues:* there, he designates himself "the man of nature" (Second Dialogue, 851/147; Third Dialogue, 939/216) and establishes an equivalence between himself and "the primitive nature of man" (Second Dialogue, 850/147). "In short, just as I found the man of nature in his books, I found in him the man of his books" (ibid., 866/159). "Where could the painter and apologist of nature, so disfigured and calumnied now, have found his model if not in his own heart? He has described it as he himself felt" (Third Dialogue, 936/214).

This establishes a continuity between Rousseau's doctrinal works and his personal writings. This is what authorizes us—even obliges us—to turn to his autobiographical works when we want to become more familiar with one of the ways of man that he has traced, that of the solitary individual. Rousseau himself lays claim to this continuity: "His system may be false, but in developing it, he portrayed himself truthfully in a manner so characteristic and so sure that it's impossible for me to mistake it" (Third Dialogue, 934/212).

Having decided that the man of nature should resemble himself, Rousseau finds himself at once judge and litigant. Suddenly, he can no longer remain impartial. Whoever plays with the two senses of "nature," "society," or "natural man" is too biased regarding the outcome of the debate. Rousseau, here, is as guilty of error as his fraternal enemies, the "philosophers,"[3] are; his mistake, though, is a mirror image of theirs. They defend doctrines that they do not bother to practice in their own lives—the irresponsibility of the modern intellectual. As for Rousseau, he expects a continuum to exist between speaking and doing, between ideal and real. Up to this point he is correct, but he wants to go further. He wants the two to coincide, and he therefore paints the ideal according to the real, since it is his everyday life and being that serve as his model. He nevertheless knows all too well that such a simplification is unacceptable: "It is necessary to know what ought to be in order to judge soundly about what is" (*Emile,* Bk. 5, 836–37/458). The hypocrisy (or cynicism, or thoughtlessness) of the "philosophers" must be condemned. But it is not therefore necessary to embrace the adversary and to eliminate the distance between ideal and real: that there is a continuum between the two does not mean that they coincide. The ideal can orient life without being mistaken for it.

Whatever else it may be, radical solitude cannot constitute an ideal for man, for the simple reason that it is impossible to achieve. What Rousseau presents to us as solitude are two complementary experiences: limited communication and the quest for the self.

As we have seen, limited communication is not solitude. How could a writer—a man who spends his life refashioning words taken from others in order to create new formulations meant for others—be an incarnation of solitude? He is in constant communication with others: a mediated communication, to be sure, but nonetheless an intense one. Yet what is Rousseau if not a writer? To what else does he devote his life? Not only does he cover thousands of pages with words, but he also knows that he thereby establishes a particularly solid kind of communication which even death will not be able to interrupt. This explains his concern,

3. See Note 1 to Chapter 2 of this volume on the meaning of "philosophers."

during his autobiographical period and even during the worst moments of his misanthropy, about his reputation and about the opinion of his future readers. "I would easily consent to have no existence at all in the memory of men, but I cannot consent, I admit it, to remain defamed. . . . But I cannot consider as something indifferent to men the reinstatement of my memory" (*Dialogues*, Third Dialogue, 953/227–28). Does a true solitary confide his manuscripts to trustworthy people, give them precise instructions, and multiply copies and precautions?

Like us all, Rousseau would like to be loved. He would like to live with others. But he was not so fated. Two factors conspired against him (whose relative weight is not particularly germane to this discussion): the hostility provoked by such an extraordinary personality, and his own suspicious character. So he withdraws into "supplements": writing, escape into the imagination, vegetative nature, people reduced to the role of instruments or objects. But at every moment, as we now know, he realizes that the substitute is not worth the original.

Yet Rousseau finds himself erecting this substitute as an ideal that accords with his decision to paint natural man after his own likeness. Here his proposal is no longer defensible. A legitimate model for autobiographical inquiry cannot furnish a common ideal, a way for man. Such an ideal must answer to criteria other than chance, the accidents that, if we are courageous enough to acknowledge the fact, make us one way rather than another. From this perspective, the "supplements" Rousseau employs are of unequal value. Even if a preference for solitude, escape into the imagination, meditation among the plants, and writing are morally neutral stances and issue from the individual's freedom (from his right), this cannot be said for depersonalizing other human beings. Yet this is what defines Rousseau's relationships with the individuals around him. To reduce others to mere auxiliaries dependent upon the self, to refuse to grant them the status of entirely separate subjects, is to renounce the equality of men. Egoism is perhaps the destiny of the individual; it should not be his ideal.

As for the quest for the self, it is difficult to present the drifting of a boat on the surface of the lake as one of the ways open to man. But this quest is accompanied by a debatable hierarchy of values. The solitary individual, abandoning all reference to others, renounces by this very fact every virtue, whether it be "civic" or "humanitarian." Rousseau does not see any drawback to this renunciation. On the contrary: "The instinct of nature is . . . certainly more secure than the law of virtue" (*Dialogues,* Second Dialogue, 864/158). Allowing our natural goodness to express itself is sufficient; the result will be the same as (or, indeed, superior to) that obtained through virtue. But is goodness itself deeply embedded enough in man? After having scrutinized himself, Rousseau must renounce his aspiration to goodness and remain contented with the happiness that can be procured by the simple satisfaction of his desires. "In my present situation, I no longer have any other rule of conduct than to follow my propensity in everything without restraint. . . . Wisdom itself wills that in what remains within my reach I do whatever gratifies me . . . without any rule other than my fancy" (*Reveries,* Seventh Walk, 1060/89).

Rousseau wants to see in this attitude "great wisdom and even great virtue" (ibid., 1061/90). But his claim is baseless. The individual can be happy by giving in to his desires; he cannot lay claim to these other qualities without having first modified the meaning of the words. Rousseau has changed greatly since those pages in the *Confessions* where he condemns this very doctrine, attributed (probably justly) to Diderot: "namely that the sole duty of man is to follow the inclinations of his heart in everything" (Bk. 9, 468/393). Emile's tutor has already warned us against the temptation to base our conduct solely on the intensity of pleasure: "he who is only good remains so only as long as he takes pleasure in being so. Goodness is broken and perishes under the impact of the human passions. The man who is only good is good only for himself"

(*Emile*, Bk. 5, 817/444). "Inform me, then, at what crime a man stops when he has only the wishes of his heart for laws and knows how to resist nothing that he desires?" (ibid.). With his habitual clairvoyance, Rousseau here envisions a path that is quite familiar to us today, the path that man—man understood as a desiring machine—is destined to take.[4] And he immediately points to its dangers. This is, nevertheless, the way taken by the solitary walker of the *Reveries*, a way that leads beyond good and evil to a cult of the intensity of experience.

To reproach Rousseau for lacking morality would require a certain naiveté. It would also ignore the fact that the *Reveries* are not addressed to others and do not describe an ideal. As for Rousseau, he has sufficiently explained himself by appealing to the exceptional circumstances that led him to make these choices. We can go further and question the status of everything he teaches us about the way of the solitary individual. Let's put aside any attempted assimilation of the ideal with the author's own life. There then remains, on the one hand, the description of a mode of life that is, after all, only a last resort, and, on the other hand, the example of a man who has not found happiness. Rousseau has explored the behavioral logic embodied by this way of life in detail; he has made it into an ideal only by way of explaining himself. Against his own will, perhaps, but not unwittingly, he shows that the way of the solitary individual does not lead to happiness and he refrains from recommending it to us.

---

4. The phrase "man understood as a desiring machine" translates *"l'homme-machine désirante,"* which refers to the "machine-man" *(l'homme machine)* described by Julien Offray de la Mettrie in his materialist tract *L'Homme machine* (1748), one of the most controversial works published in Rousseau's time.

CHAPTER 4

The Moral Individual

THE THIRD WAY

Let us return to our starting point. In the initial dichotomy that Rousseau establishes between the state of nature and the state of society, the first term is more desirable, but only as an ideal existence. Had it in fact once existed, it would still be impossible to return to it. As for the second term, it is real, but less desirable: it describes life as it is led around us. This is why it is necessary to find a way to break this impasse. The citizen pursues the first way: he becomes fully aware of the reality of the second term—i.e., the fact that man is irreversibly a social creature. Having renounced the initial ideal, considered beyond his reach, the citizen creates another, purely social one: it is therefore necessary to erase all trace of our original aspirations, to denature man thoroughly. As we have already seen, the result of this voluntarist attitude is disappointing. The solitary individual chooses a second way: he fully adheres to the ideal of natural man. Yet he then finds himself forced to set aside human sociability, imagining that living alone will allow him to rediscover the state of nature. Such blindness could never, in its turn, lead to lasting happiness. Both paths thus carry significant risks that one might hesitate to take. Rousseau discreetly warns us against the first, all the while illustrating—at times unwillingly—the dilemmas of the second.

Here, then, is the problem: how can we reconcile man's reality (his sociability) with his ideal (his "naturalness"), since the elimination of either of the terms inevitably leads to an impasse? "If perchance the double object we set for ourselves could be joined in a single one by removing the contradictions of man, a great obstacle to his happiness would be removed" (*Emile*, Bk. 1, 251/41). Rousseau attempts the reconciliation of these two opposing terms— the integration of the natural ideal with social reality—in *Emile*, the work he himself considers the high point of his writings. Just as the systematic treatise proved to be an adequate genre to describe the way of the citizen and autobiography was the appropriate genre for discussing the way of the solitary individual, a specific literary genre is appropriate for discussing the moral individual. *Emile* is a mixed work, at once personal and impersonal, fiction and reflection. It is a treatise on the formation of the ideal man (a "natural" one, in accordance with Rousseau's terminology) in the bosom of society. "Although I want to form the man of nature, the object is not, for all that, to make him a savage and to relegate him to the depths of the woods" (Bk. 4, 550/255). "There is a great difference between the natural man living in the state of nature and the natural man living in the state of society. Emile is not a savage to be relegated to the desert. He is a savage made to inhabit cities" (ibid., 483–84/205). The two meanings of the expression "natural man," which the solitary individual tends to confound, are here clearly distinguished.

The first way open to man leads him to the "social whole." This is the way of socialism, we might say, in the literal sense of the word. The second way open to him wants to enclose him in the "individual whole"; this, then, is the way of individualism.[1] Rousseau does not have a specific name for the third way. In honor of

---

1. The previous two sentences are meant to echo Rousseau's formulation in

Montesquieu, to whom Rousseau is curiously close on this point, we might call it the way of moderation. This is Montesquieu's label for a type of "government" marked by a certain mixture in the partition of powers. Although he dreams of unity, Rousseau nevertheless can see himself as he truly is: "My mixed being," he says of himself in the *Letter to Franquières* (*O.C.*, Vol. 4, 1139).[2] Moreover, his character Emile is the product of this same mixture on the level of the individual. Rather than trying to "denature" man, an effort will instead be made to adapt his nature to society as it exists, and to bring his own existence closer to the ideal.

There is, then, another way in which Rousseau will envision the unavoidable fact of society and its relationship to the individual. First of all, it is essential to understand that the individual man really has no choice. "By leaving the state of nature, we force our fellows to leave it, too. No one can remain in it in spite of the others" (*Emile*, Bk. 3, 467/193). If one stubbornly tries to live in society as if it did not exist—in other words, if one chooses solitude—one is condemned to failure. "A man who wanted to regard himself as an isolated being, not dependent at all on anything and sufficient unto himself, could only be miserable" (ibid.) When he so chooses, Rousseau does not at all confound two radically different kinds of solitude: one that belongs only to the state of nature and another that is possible in society.

In society (that is, everywhere), the self-sufficient being is miserable. God alone is happy as a self-sufficient being, and man is not a god. "God alone enjoys an absolute happiness. But who among us has the idea of it? If some imperfect being could suffice unto himself, what would he enjoy according to us? He would be alone; he would be miserable" (ibid., Bk. 4, 503/221). When looking through the eyes of the solitary individual, Rousseau sees only

---

Emile of the contrast between "natural man" and "civil man" (Bk. 1, 249/39–40), quoted above.

2. "My mixed being" translates *"Moi être mixte,"* which also might be translated "Me, a mixed being."

the negative aspects of urban life. Yet, when he thinks after the fashion of his moderate man, he understands urbanity's attraction perfectly well. "If each man were self-sufficient, the only important thing for him to know would be the land capable of providing him with subsistence." So too for the savage. "But for us to whom civil life is necessary and who can no longer get along without devouring men, our interest is to frequent the countries where the most men are found. This is why all flock to Rome, Paris, and London" (ibid., Bk. 5, 831/454).

A passage from the *Dialogues* clearly confirms this alternate view of sociality. It is all the more telling, as it follows a description of Rousseau's own personal taste for solitude. But, when he wishes to do so, Rousseau is perfectly capable of distinguishing the particularities of his life from his ideal for man. He therefore writes: "absolute solitude is a state that is sad and contrary to nature: affectionate feelings nurture the soul, communication of ideas enlivens the mind. Our sweetest existence is relative and collective, and our true *self* is not entirely within us" (Second Dialogue, 813/118).

Solitude is not contrary to the state of nature but to the nature of man such as he really exists, that is, in society. "One must not confound what is natural in the savage state with what is natural in the civil state" (*Emile*, Bk. 5, 764/406). The *Reveries* recall, with melancholy, that the others are always within the self. But here in *Emile*, Rousseau affirms rather euphorically that a part of the self resides in others. Our happiness is therefore that of a social being; even from an egoistic point of view, the "other" is indispensable. Society, then, is not a lesser evil, a supplement; it is the source of qualities that do not exist without it. And communication is, in itself, a virtue.

DOMESTIC EDUCATION

In order to repair the rupture between nature and society, Rousseau proposes a method of reconciliation that he calls domestic education, which differs from civic education. Civic education has the good of society in sight, and it focuses on the group. Domestic education aims at the improvement of the individual and is dedicated to him. But since man lives in society, this improvement consists precisely in preparing him for social life: "the most necessary art for a man and a citizen, which is knowing how to live with his fellows" (*Emile*, Bk. 4, 655/328). Unfortunately, this is not how education is usually practiced: "They claim they form us for society, and they instruct us as if each of us were going to spend his life in thinking alone in his cell" (ibid., 543/2490). It is this deficiency that is to be remedied by *Emile; or, On Education*—a book that remains at the same time an extended reflection on fundamental principles rather than a manual addressed to educators.

The means Rousseau finds to overcome the tension between the state of nature and the state of society is actually quite simple. He conceives of education in two long phases, each of which will emphasize either one or the other of these two antithetical terms. The first phase, which Rousseau calls "negative education," spans the period between birth and "the age of reason," or about fifteen years of age. The second phase, that of social education, begins at this point and ends only at death. The goal of the first is the development of "the natural man" in us, while the goal of the second is to adapt us to life with other human beings. During the first phase, Emile will learn "all that relates to himself"; during the second, he will come to know "relations" and will acquire "social virtues" (ibid., Bk. 3, 488/208). Natural man knows relationships only with things, while the ideal of the citizen is in turn to reestablish proper relationships with men. This will also be the principle of the first phase of education, but not of the second. "So long as he knows himself only in his physical being, he ought to study himself in his relations with things. This is the task of his childhood. When he begins to sense his moral being, he ought to study himself in his relations with men. This is the job of his whole life" (ibid., Bk. 4, 493/214). "The child observes things while waiting to be able to observe men. The man ought to begin by observing his kind and then observe things if he has time" (ibid., Bk. 5, 832/454–55).

Education for the individual will therefore be directed, before all else, toward the physical being; it will help exercise the senses and perfect the organs. On the material plane, it will try to make the infant autonomous (and is the contrary of "infantilization"): in order to accomplish his will, he has no need "to put another's arms at the end of his own" (ibid., Bk. 2, 309/84). Clearly, this autonomy is not equivalent to self-sufficiency, the ideal of the solitary individual. The latter is the goal of adult life, and it deals with our moral rather than physical being.

Since the infant is the object of many lessons other than those lavished upon him by his teacher, an important part of this effort must be devoted to preventing these other kinds of knowledge, other kinds of demands, from taking root. Hence Rousseau's reason for calling this education "negative." It is useless to bother about social relations, or moral qualities, or the abstract operations of the mind (for we have not yet entered the "age of reason"). It is equally futile to have the child read books—with the sole and telling exception of *Robinson Crusoe*, in which the hero lives as a "natural man" on his island.

If the autonomous development of the child is thus nurtured, all the while holding social pressures at bay, the result will be the formation of an individual whose greatest quality will be authenticity, that is, a certain coherence with himself. It is necessary that Emile "see with his eyes, that he feel with his heart, that no authority govern him beyond that of his own reason" (ibid., Bk. 4, 551/255). He will have learned not to avoid sociability but instead to avoid the slavish submission to current opinion, the need to act in accordance with current yet ever-changing norms, and the concern for what the crowd may think of him ("what will they say about you?"). Just as sociability need not become vanity, so too solitude is not egoism. A person educated in this spirit will act "without worrying about arbitrary evaluations whose only law is fashion or prejudice" (ibid., Bk. 4, 670/339). In a word, this individual will always prefer reason and informed judgment to authority—be it political, social, or familial, be it overtly exercised or underhanded. It is through the exercise of reason, however purely individual, that human beings communicate with their species.

WISDOM

Yet, with this formation of the individual, domestic education is only half-complete. "Emile is not made to remain always solitary. As a member of society, he ought to fulfill its duties. Since he is made to live with men, he ought to know them" (*Emile*, Bk. 4, 654/327). This second stage is by far the most important. "Up to now our care has only been a child's game. It takes on true importance only at present. This period, when ordinary educations end, is properly the one when ours ought to begin" (ibid., Bk. 4, 490/212).

If two kinds of education are necessary, it is because human actions must undergo a double test and be judged by two different scales of value. Coming at the end of our individual education is the first test, which concerns the authenticity of our conduct. Here, the best action is perfectly at one with our being and eventually achieves the highest possible degree of intensity. The criterion of judgment is immanent in each particular being, and this is the only one known by the solitary individual. This particular quality is necessary but not sufficient: an evil individual, after all, can be perfectly at one with himself ("do as you will"), and thus authentic. Moreover, he might work toward accomplishing evil with great intensity, and this will be no less an evil. It is at this point that the second test comes in, a test prepared by social education. Actions must now satisfy transcendental criteria that are common to all beings. This is the apprenticeship in good and evil—that is, in morality—that can take place only in the context of interpersonal relationships.

If there is one doctrinal point about which Rousseau never changed his mind, it is most certainly that in the state of nature, where there is no communication among men, there is no way of distinguishing between virtue and vice. The sentiment of justice is unknown there, and morality is absent. Human beings, then, are not yet fully human in that state. "Limited to physical instinct alone, he is nothing, he is a beast" (*Letter to Beaumont, O.C.,* Vol. 4, 936). Only human interaction develops reason and the moral sense that rests upon it. "It is only by becoming sociable that he becomes a moral being" (Political Fragments, 477/19). There is no doubt about the judgment to be made of this transition; it is "the happy moment . . . that changed him from a stupid, limited animal into an intelligent being and a man" (*Social Contract,* Bk. 1, Chap. 8, 364/141).

These two phases of education correspond to the two "states" of humanity. During the first phase, the isolated individual and his physical capacities are emphasized; any and all appeals to reason and morality must therefore be put aside. It is during the second phase that man, having learned about social relations and acquired reason, can discover "the notions of good and evil which truly constitute him as a man and an integral part of his species" (*Emile,* Bk. 4, 501/220).

But it is no more the goal of social education to produce a citizen, in the sense Rousseau gives to the word, than it is the ideal of the first phase of our education to create a solitary individual. The third way is not realized by mechanically adding elements taken from the first two ways. Human society is here understood in its broadest sense: it is no longer a matter of a single country but the entire species. Recall the parallel between Socrates and Cato. Socrates, who inhabited the entire world, was the incarnation of moral virtue, or wisdom. Cato, the patriot, embodied greatness, or civic virtue. Emile's goal will also be to gain entry into "the age of wisdom" (*Emile,* First Version [Favre Version], Preamble, *O.C.,* Vol. 4, 60).

Not only do virtue and morality exist only in society, but they are also, in fact, the recognition of the existence of others. They are defined by the possibility of extending the same attitude to all of mankind; only that which is universalizable is moral. "The less the object of our care is immediately involved with us, the less the illusion of particular interest is to be feared. The more one generalizes this interest, the more it becomes equitable, and the love of mankind is nothing other than the love of justice" (*Emile,* Bk. 4, 547/252). Human wisdom is not the quest for but rather the forgetting of oneself. "The more his cares are consecrated to the happiness of others, the more they will be enlightened and wise and the less he will be deceived about what is good or bad" (ibid., 547–48/252). It is in this manner that the Savoyard Vicar identifies the good man and the wicked man with the altruist and the egoist. "The good man orders himself in relation to the whole, and the wicked one orders the whole in relation to himself. The latter makes himself the center of all things; the former measures his radius and keeps to the circumference" (ibid., 602/292). And while the citizen should avoid overly intimate contact with foreigners (and the solitary individual with *all* men), the moral individual will travel beyond his fatherland: "It is also an excellent precaution against the empire of national prejudices" (ibid., Bk. 5, 855/471).

In Rousseau's thought, this universalist attitude is tied to Christianity. Recall that Jesus appeared in the place of Socrates: "healthy ideas of natural right and the brotherhood of all men were disseminated rather late and made such slow progress in the world that it was only Christianity that generalized them sufficiently" (*Social Contract,* First Version, Bk. 1, Chap. 2, 287/81). Rousseau's theism, which is a universal religion, aspires to "a morality made for humanity" (*Letter to Beaumont,* 969), to "general principles common to all men" (ibid., 971).

The moral individual is not the citizen. What, then, is his relationship to the civic ideal? Initially, Rousseau recommends caution and patience to him. Until we come to know all the elements of a particular situation, let us submit to the laws of the country in which we live without trying to modify them. All change is bad in itself, and should be undertaken only as a last resort. The first reaction is therefore conservative. Yet, little by little, we come to understand more deeply the political regime under which we live. In order to do so, we need an absolute standard ("ought" will come before "is"). This standard can be found in Rousseau's very own *Social Contract,* a work that is summarized within *Emile.* Here, the function of this reflection on the ideal city becomes clear: it is not a program for action, but an analytical tool. "Our first concern was to establish the true principles of political right. Now that our foundations are laid, come and examine what men have built on them" (*Emile,* Bk. 5, 849/ 467).

Real political regimes will never conform to the schema in the *Social Contract.* But there are degrees of divergence, and the degree determines the moral individual's attitude toward institutions. "What difference does it make that the social contract has not been observed, if individual interest protected him as the general will would have done, if public violence guaranteed him against individual violence, if the evil he saw done made him love what is good, and if our institutions themselves have made him know and hate their own iniquities" (ibid., Bk. 5, 858/473). Unlike the solitary individual, the moral individual is not indifferent to the institutions of the country in which he lives, but he does not ask that they be perfect; he does not seek the ideal rather than the real. He does not expect them to make him free. It is up to him alone to win his liberty. He does, however, require a certain minimum: that these institutions protect and guard him against acts of violence by individuals, so that he can live a "tranquil" life. A particular society is acceptable (without thereby being ideal) if it allows its members to develop their critical reason—in other words, if it permits them to distinguish between the ideal and the real, rather than requiring them to call it an earthly paradise. Only the deluded think that they dwell in the realm of "the good," but the good can serve as a measure for one's actions. Here we see how far Rousseau's ideas on life in society are from the totalitarian program for which he has at times been held responsible. It is only when these basic liberties are not guaranteed that the individual should reject his society, whether by revolt or by exile.

The moral individual will therefore live in society, but he will not totally alienate himself to *a* society. He will respect his State but devote himself to humanity—not, as we have seen, to suffering peoples unknown to him on the other side of the world, but to those near and dear to him. Through these ties with others the individual will exercise his universal spirit, and therefore his virtue. Emile will not be a statesman; he will marry and cherish his loved ones. But unlike the ideal of the solitary individual, the couple's ideal is no longer complete fusion, and hence the disappearance of the other: "Let each of you remain master of his own person and his caresses and have the right to dispense them to the other only at his own will" (*Emile*, Bk. 5, 863/477). Each keeps his own will free; the other is thus a subject in his own right—an affirmation all the more stunning when one recalls that Rousseau is elsewhere against the equality of the sexes.

These are a few of the characteristics of the third way open to man—that of the moral individual. Rousseau himself did not always follow this path, and yet it is the only one he recommends without hesitation. It does not automatically lead to happiness; and, when it does, this happiness promises neither absolute certainty nor definitive rest. It consists of practicing a healthy form of sociability: it is not much, perhaps, but it is all that is open to us. As Rousseau remarks, we draw the remedy from the very nature of our disease, and do so in a way that most closely conforms to our human condition. "It is man's weakness which makes him sociable; it is our common miseries which turn our hearts to humanity," he writes in *Emile* (Bk. 4, 503/221), adding: "Thus from our very infirmity is born our frail happiness."

Chronological List of Works by Rousseau (1712–1778) Cited in the Text

1749	*Discourse on the Sciences and Arts (First Discourse)*
1751	*Observations* (on a criticism of the *First Discourse*)
1752	*Final Reply* (to a critic of the *First Discourse*)
1754	*Discourse on the Origin of Inequality (Second Discourse)*
1755	*Letter to Philopolis* (concerning the *Second Discourse*)
	Political Economy
	Essay on the Origin of Languages
1756–57	*Writings on the Abbé de Saint-Pierre*
1754–60	Political Fragments
1758	*Julie, or The New Heloise*
1759	*Emile* (First Version)
1760	*On the Social Contract* (First Version or "Geneva Manuscript")
1761	*On the Social Contract*
	Emile
1756–62	"My Portrait"
1756–78	"The Art of Enjoyment"
1762	*Letters to Malesherbes*
	Letter to Beaumont

Major Secondary Works Consulted

Bloom, A. Introduction to *Politics and the Arts (Letter to d'Alembert)*, by Jean-Jacques Rousseau. The Free Press, 1960.

———. Introduction to *Emile*, by Jean-Jacques Rousseau. Basic Books, 1979.

Burgelin, P. "L'unité dans l'œuvre de J.-J. Rousseau." *Revue de métaphysique et morale* (1960).

Derathé, R. *Jean-Jacques Rousseau et la science politique de son temps*. Vrin, 1970.

———. "Montesquieu et J.-J. Rousseau." *Revue internationale de philosophie* 9 (1955).

———. "L'unité de la pensée de J.-J. Rousseau." In *J.-J. Rousseau*, edited by S. Baud-Bovy et al. La Baconnière, 1962.

Derrida, J. *De la grammatologie*. Minuit, 1967. [Available as *Of Grammatology*, translated by Gayatri Chakravorty Spivak. Baltimore: Johns Hopkins University Press, 1974. *Eds.*]

Goldschmidt, V. *Anthropologie et politique: Les Principes du système de Rousseau*. Vrin, 1974.

———. *Écrits*. Vol. 2. Vrin, 1984.

Gouhier, H. *Les Méditations métaphysiques de J.-J. Rousseau*. Vrin, 1970.

Groethuysen, B. *Jean-Jacques Rousseau*. Gallimard, 1949.

Jouvenel, B. de. "Essai sur la politique de Rousseau." In *Du contrat social,* by Jean-Jacques Rousseau. Le livre de poche, 1978. (This essay is accompanied by two others by Jouvenel on Rousseau.)

Lejeune, P. *Le Pacte autobiographique.* Le Seuil, 1975.

Masters, R. D. *The Political Philosophy of Rousseau.* Princeton University Press, 1968.

May, G. *Rousseau par lui-même.* Le Seuil, 1961.

Munteano. *Solitude et contradictions de Jean-Jacques Rousseau.* Nizet, 1975.

Pensée de Rousseau. Le Seuil, 1984. (Contains writings on Rousseau by E. Weil, E. Cassirer, L. Strauss, C. Eisenmann, R. Derathé, P. Bénichou, and V. Goldschmidt.)

Philonenko, A. *J.-J. Rousseau et la pensée du malheur.* 3 vols. Vrin, 1984.

Polin, R. *La Politique de la solitude.* Sirey, 1971.

Rang, M. "L'éducation publique et la formation des citoyens chez J.-J. Rousseau." In *Études sur le Contrat social.* Les Belles Lettres, 1964.

Ricatte, R. *Réflexions sur les* Rêveries. José Corti, 1960.

Starobinski, J. *La Transparence et l'obstacle.* Gallimard, 1971.

Strauss, L. *Droit naturel et histoire.* Plon, 1964.

V. Goldschmidt's writings on Rousseau have been particularly useful for me.